Leading the Campaign

Part of the American Council on Education
Series on Higher Education
Susan Slesinger, Executive Editor

Other selected titles in the series:

Leading the Campaign

Advancing Colleges and Universities

Michael J. Worth

Published in partnership with the

AMERICAN COUNCIL ON EDUCATION
® The Unifying Voice for Higher Education

ROWMAN & LITTLEFIELD PUBLISHERS, INC.
Lanham • New York • Toronto • Plymouth, UK

Published in partnership with the American Council on Education

Published by Rowman & Littlefield
A wholly owned subsidiary of The Rowman & Littlefield Publishing Group, Inc.
4501 Forbes Boulevard, Suite 200, Lanham, Maryland 20706
http://www.rowmaneducation.com

Estover Road, Plymouth PL6 7PY, United Kingdom

British Library Cataloguing in Publication Information Available

Library of Congress Cataloging-in-Publication Data
Worth, Michael J.
  Leading the campaign : advancing colleges and universities / Michael J. Worth.
     p. cm. — (The American Council on Education series on higher education)
  Includes bibliographical references and index.
  ISBN 978-1-60709-649-8 (cloth : alk. paper) — ISBN 978-1-60709-651-1
(electronic : alk. paper)
  1. Educational fund raising—United States. 2. Educational leadership—United
States. 3. State universities and colleges—United States—Finance. I. Title.
Leadership LB2336.W69 2010
     371.2'06—dc22

                                                              2009041669

Printed in the United States of America

x c
$47.25
0=456551350

Contents

Introduction

This book was written in late 2008 and the first half of 2009, as the daily news brought reports of gyrating markets, increasing unemployment, and college and university campaigns struggling to make progress in the face of economic crisis and uncertainty. But, for the most part, I have chosen to ignore the current economic climate, not knowing what it may be by the time of publication and confident as well that it will be improved at some point in the future. So, this is not a book about campaigns in hard times. It is just about campaigns.

Chapter 1 includes a brief history of campaigns in higher education. That history reveals that the model has endured depressions and recessions, wars, and other national crises over more than a century. It is an approach to educational fundraising that is rooted in fundamentals of human nature and values that do not change as frequently as economic cycles. The campaign model has evolved and methods have changed over the decades, but its central principles have proven to be effective under a variety of circumstances. This book focuses on those central principles, with recognition that they may need to be adapted to new realities in the future.

Some say that today's entrepreneurial donors have a new perspective and that they do not respond to campaigns as much as donors in previous decades. This book also addresses that question and makes the case that campaigns may be adaptable to meet the inclinations of donors as well as economic trends.

Much of the material in this book represents the wisdom of practitioners who have written about campaigns and created an abundant literature. There are also some findings from research, many of which substantiate practitioner wisdom and some which challenge it. And, the book includes my own views on a number of points, with which some may disagree.

This is not a professional autobiography, although I include a number of examples from my experience as a development officer and consultant to illustrate certain points. That experience encompasses more than thirty-five years and began with an unexpected introduction to fundraising under highly unusual circumstances. It offered some vivid lessons that are still relevant. I recount the story here to establish those enduring points.

In the fall of 1971 I had completed a graduate degree and was in search of employment on a campus. I had no investments and owned no property, beyond my car, so I was in most ways not that aware of general economic conditions. In retrospect, I realize they were bad. The economy was in recession and academic positions were not exactly plentiful. During my search, I had occasion to speak with the president of my undergraduate alma mater, Wilkes College (now Wilkes University), in Wilkes-Barre, Pennsylvania. The president, Francis J. Michelini, whom I had known from my undergraduate days, made me an attractive offer. I would work half-time in his office as assistant to the president, helping him with "administrative and board matters," and would teach two undergraduate sections of Economics 101.

I accepted the position and started in September 1971. It was an enjoyable and productive academic year, a wonderful learning experience for a young man. It provided my first exposure to higher education administration and the work of the board of trustees (which I barely knew existed when I was an undergraduate). It was going well until June of 1972.

That month, Hurricane Agnes, later downgraded to a tropical storm, moved up over the East Coast, dumping inches of saturating rain. It became essentially stationary over upstate New York for several days and poured heavy rain into tributaries of the Susquehanna River. The river gradually rose to a record height of more than forty feet, and on June 23, 1972, the levees protecting the city of Wilkes-Barre gave way. Rushing floodwaters decimated some portions of the city and its suburbs, cut the community in two, and covered many buildings to the rooftop. That included the fifty-eight buildings on the campus of Wilkes College, which was set along the banks of the river near downtown Wilkes-Barre.

Having been evacuated from my home and with the city secured by the National Guard, it was many days before I could make my way back to the campus. Crews were already at work and the scenes were horrifying. A crane was removing destroyed grand pianos through a hole in the roof of the performing arts center, and a backhoe was pushing the mushy remains of books out of a hole in the wall of the recently constructed library. The wooden floor of the gymnasium had buckled into three-foot-high waves the length of the court. There were inches of mud and the sounds of pumps moving water out of basements everywhere.

I met President Michelini, who was walking the campus in boots and jeans, stopping to give encouragement or direction to some of the crews at work. We had a conversation and he explained, "If we're not open by September, we're out of business. The students will not return and the faculty will be looking for new positions." It was then mid-July. "The estimated damage is about $20 million," he went on, "money we do not have." This was, of course, in 1972 dollars. Without knowing how he would pay the bills, Michelini had signed contracts to have the campus restored with an intensive effort, a program he named Operation Snapback. "Somehow," he said, "we will just need to figure out a way to get the money." It was do or die.

There was not much for me to do by way of my usual administrative work, especially without phones or electric power, and it was the summer, so I was not in the classroom. The college's development office was small, essentially consisting of one person, the director of development, Tom Kelly. Michelini suggested that I "go over and work with Tom" to see what together we might be able to accomplish in raising philanthropic funds to save the college. "I need to stay here to oversee the recovery effort," he said, "but I also will be working on some other avenues." And so Tom Kelly and I set up shop on the top floor of the administration building, powered eventually by a generator and a single temporary phone line and fed by the Red Cross truck that had set up relief services down the street. We devoted our combined efforts to saving our institution, from which both of us had graduated just a few years before.

In the weeks that followed we would call, write, and travel to visit foundations, companies, alumni, and other individuals, pounding the pavements of New York and Philadelphia with vivid photographs of the devastation and pleas for support of rebuilding. There was much sympathy for the cause, but also some hesitation. Some asked, "What if the campus cannot be restored in time?" "What if the students all go somewhere else and do not return in September?" "What happens if you raise only part of the money; will the college go bankrupt?" All good questions, but apparently we were sufficiently persuasive and confident to secure commitments for at least a few million dollars.

A friend of the college, William Scranton, who was a former governor of Pennsylvania, opened doors for us in Pittsburgh. He reminded some of that city's leading citizens that he had indeed been helpful to one of their local universities during his term as governor and suggested that they now might wish to help a stricken institution in his part of the state. They responded. Other friends of the college and members of its board were similarly helpful. Through all of these efforts, we had raised, by my recollection, several million dollars by the beginning of September. The physical restoration of the campus had proceeded at an amazing rate, but we still had not raised enough to pay the full bill.

Then on September 9, 1972, a helicopter brought the president of the United States, Richard Nixon, to the campus to hand President Michelini a federal government check covering the balance of what was needed. It turned out that Michelini had indeed been pursuing some other avenues, via our congressman, the ironically named Daniel J. Flood, who happened to be a senior member of the House Committee on Appropriations.

The campus opened in September, the students returned, the college survived, and I had found my calling as a college fundraiser. I later went on to other institutions, eventually serving as director of development at the University of Maryland–College Park for seven years, and then vice president for development and alumni affairs at The George Washington University for eighteen years. Tom Kelly moved on as well, serving as dean of the business school and then for many years as vice president for development at Binghamton University, where he remains as a member of the faculty.

Obviously, my first experience with higher education fundraising was anything but typical. Few institutions will ever face the existential threat that Wilkes endured in 1972, although surely some institutions on the Gulf Coast did so years later following Hurricane Katrina.

This fundraising effort was not a campaign, because it did not meet several of the defining criteria, discussed in chapter 1 of this book. But, atypical as it was, my first experience with fundraising did provide some lessons that I found to be of lasting value and, with modification, still applicable under more normal circumstances in subsequent years.

First, donors respond to real needs. People act when it is necessary and important to do so. It is impossible to duplicate the story we had to tell or the heartbreaking photos of devastation that we carried with us in that effort and it is surely not possible, or desirable, to create a crisis for the purpose of raising money. But it remains true that individuals respond more forcefully to needs that are tangible and urgent than to the hypothetical, common, or mundane. Few institutions of higher education will ever face a similar situation, but their fundraising will nevertheless succeed to the extent that they can present a case that is visual and real. As this book discusses in a later chapter, too many campaigns proceed with humdrum cases that fail to create either excitement or urgency.

Second, as we experienced even under the unique circumstances of a disaster, people do want assurance that their money will be well spent toward achievable ends. The case needs to be credible and goals plausible. The possibility that their gifts might have been money down the drain if the college failed to accomplish its challenging goal of recovery did, understandably, give pause to some whom we approached. Even under normal circumstances, donors will respond to realistic goals but look with skepticism on overly ambitious ones. People give alongside others if they have confidence that the overall program can be accomplished but usually do not want to act alone in pursuing a pipe dream. That was certainly true in 1972 and it is ever more so today, when many donors view their giving as an investment in a plan that needs to be both logical and achievable.

The *third* lesson of my unusual first experience is that institutional friends matter, especially those who have influence and favors to be called in. Without the intervention of the former governor and other trustees and friends, we would never have been able to raise funds from philanthropists in other regions of the state. Without the influence of our local congressman, it is unlikely that the federal funds would have been provided. No amount of earnestness and persuasiveness on our part alone could have opened enough doors or bank accounts. No level of effort or charisma would have been sufficient without powerful allies of long standing.

Fourth and finally, leadership is crucial. I learned a lot about leadership from President Michelini in those trying days. Whatever personal doubts he may have held about the college's ability to recover and survive, he was unswerving in his outward confidence, optimism, and determination that it would be saved and continue to thrive. Faced with the personal crises of damaged homes, lost property, and uncertainty about their future livelihoods, many people were inspired by his leadership to pull together to successfully meet an enormous challenge. Creating inspiration and confidence is the essence of presidential leadership and it is as necessary under ordinary circumstances as it was under the extraordinary events of 1972 in Wilkes-Barre, Pennsylvania.

I have served six presidents in a staff capacity and others in my role as a consultant. I am convinced that the most effective *fundraising* presidents are those who are first and foremost visionary and committed *leaders of their institutions*.

In the following chapters, I summarize some time-tested principles of educational fundraising and campaigns. Consistent with the book's sponsorship by the American Council on Education, there is an emphasis on the leadership role of the president in the campaign and on the critical decisions that ultimately fall to the president. Fundraising may come naturally for some presidents and maybe not for others. Fundraising skills can be developed and/or other people can help to offset whatever shortcomings the president may have in that area. But confident and visionary institutional leadership can only come from the president, and such leadership is the sine qua non of successful fundraising.

From the vantage point of this writing, it is difficult to know what will be the condition of the U.S. and world economies by the time this book is read. Perhaps we will be in an economic recovery with increasing philanthropy and the announcement of higher campaign goals. Or perhaps we will be in recession, with campaigns on hold, extended, or scaled down. But colleges and universities are enduring institutions. Support for them has grown most years despite recessions, wars, and other catastrophic events. They are anchors in a sea of change, and their resilience has been demonstrated time and again. Even when threatened with extinction, colleges have survived, even thrived. And the campaign has been, for more than a century, a principal strategy by which they have been advanced. That is likely to remain true in the decades ahead.

1

The Comprehensive Campaign

In 1641 William Hibbens, Hugh Peter, and Thomas Weld set sail from America to London on a mission to raise funds for a struggling young educational institution in Massachusetts. Bearing what may have been the first example of fundraising literature, a brochure entitled *New England's First Fruits*, this team solicited support for the purpose of "educating the heathen Indian," a cause that was deemed worthy by wealthy British citizens of the time. Their efforts were met with mixed results. As historian Scott Cutlip reports, Weld remained in England and never returned to America. So, too, in a way, did Peter, who was hanged there for crimes he committed under British law. Only Hibbens returned to Massachusetts, a year later, with £500 for Harvard College. As Cutlip observes, "Such were the rewards of early fund raisers" (Cutlip, 1965, p. 4).

Today's higher education leaders might say that raising funds for a college or university is still a daunting challenge and that the risk of being hanged in the process (at least figuratively) remains. But, while it remains a combination of art and science, fundraising has become considerably more systematic since the early adventures of Hibbens, Peter, and Weld. Modern campaigns are well planned, highly organized, and tightly managed initiatives that follow principles and a process developed and refined over more than a century.

This book discusses fundamental campaign principles, but is not intended as a how-to guide. Rather, its emphasis is on the strategic decisions that a campaign requires and on campaign leadership. It likely will be of interest to trustees, advancement professionals, and others concerned with the future of colleges and universities. But, consistent with its sponsorship

1

by the American Council on Education, this book emphasizes the campaign leadership of presidents.

The ability to lead a campaign is essential to success for today's college or university president. And campaign experience at some level is generally now a prerequisite credential for presidential candidates, as well as deans and other academic leaders, on both public and private campuses. Indeed, in a 2009 interview, executive search consultant R. William Funk advised aspiring presidents to gain experience in three areas that he described as most important to search committees: fundraising, athletics, and external relations. He suggested that faculty members or deans who are interested in moving to a presidency participate in a campaign and associate themselves with committees that are focused on fundraising (Masterson, 2009).

The formal period of a typical campaign encompasses seven to eight years, but pre-campaign institutional planning and post-campaign analysis and reporting can easily occupy an additional year or two. Thus, the entire process roughly coincides with the average tenure of a college or university president—8.5 years in 2008 (American Council on Education, 2008)—and successful completion of a campaign often represents one of his or her most tangible achievements. And campaigns have become about more than money, often encompassing important goals related to institutional image, visibility, and brand. The themes and goals advanced in a campaign often embody the vision and priorities that define a presidency. The campaign thus has become a principal strategy for advancing education and its institutions.

FROM BEGGING TO ADVANCEMENT STRATEGY

Many people still refer to any college or university campaign as a "capital campaign." It is a term familiar to most people and, since capital projects are among the featured objectives of most campaigns, it is not entirely inaccurate. But most campaigns today are comprehensive, encompassing capital projects as well as endowment, annual giving, and support restricted to specific current programs. Most campaigns encompass all gifts and commitments for all purposes over a defined period of years—they are umbrellas over all fundraising efforts of the institution. How we got to this model—the history of campaigns in higher education—is an interesting story worth understanding. It demonstrates how the concept of a campaign has adapted to encompass significant changes in higher education, patterns of wealth, the economy, and society.

In the nation's early centuries, fundraising for higher education was primitive by today's standards. It consisted mostly of "passing the church plate, of staging church suppers or bazaars, and writing 'begging letters'" (Cutlip, 1965, p. 7). Indeed, since many early colleges were related to a sponsoring church, their presidents were often clergy and appeals for funds often reflected a religious tone. In that period, the case for support of American colleges often was based on the desire to advance Christianity and prepare young men for the ministry (Cutlip, 1965, p. 3).

But the seeds of an organized approach can be found in some early efforts. For example, Benjamin Franklin's often-quoted advice to Gilbert Thomas on raising funds for the Presbyterian church in Philadelphia suggested campaign principles that are still employed:

> In the first place, I advise you to apply to all those whom you know will give something; next to those whom you are uncertain whether they will give anything or not, and show them the list of those who have given; and lastly, do not neglect those whom you are sure will give nothing, for in some of them you may be mistaken. (Cutlip, 1965, p. 6)

However, despite Franklin's suggestion of a method, fundraising before the twentieth century was primarily a personal transaction between asker and giver and involved far more art than science. The revolution in fundraising came in the first decade of the twentieth century, and it began outside of higher education.

The Historical Capital Campaign

In 1902, YMCA executive Lyman L. Pierce launched a campaign to raise $300,000 toward construction of a new building in Washington, DC. By 1905, he had come within $80,000 of that goal, but the campaign had stalled. Pierce called for help from another YMCA executive who had built a reputation as a successful fund raiser, Charles Sumner Ward from Chicago. Ward came to Washington to help rejuvenate the campaign, which he successfully completed. As Cutlip (1965, p. 44) describes, "The collaboration of Ward and Pierce produced the first modern fund-raising campaign techniques: careful organization, picked leadership spurred on by team competition, prestige leaders, powerful publicity, a large gift to be matched, careful records, report meetings, and a definite time limit."

The process that Ward introduced subsequently became known as the Ward method and encompassed many of the techniques that characterize a campaign today, with modifications and refinements developed by many other practitioners since.

Ward's contribution was not only the introduction of specific fundraising practices, but also the very idea that adherence to a system and skill in management are more important than personal charisma in defining a successful fund raiser (Cutlip, 1965, p. 9). Ward's approach to fundraising was focused on management of the process and the application of insights about human psychology and sociology, rather than the begging that had characterized such efforts in earlier times.

Following his success with the YMCA, Ward was retained by the University of Pittsburgh to manage a campaign for $3 million, bringing his method into higher education. Some of the people whom Ward hired to work with him in Pittsburgh subsequently founded their own fundraising firms that extended Ward's approach to college and university campaigns across the country in the following decades. Indeed, until about the mid-1960s, most campaigns were directed by consultants from such firms, who would take up residence on campus for a period of months to guide the president and volunteers through the intensive portion of the campaign, and then move on to a new assignment elsewhere. It was a model, and a lifestyle, that gave rise to some influential and colorful personalities of organized fundraising's early days. And, perhaps, it established an image of fundraising professionals that some still hold—as operators at the margins of academic institutions rather than as full partners with their campus colleagues.

Beginning in about the mid-1960s—and at an accelerating pace over the next four decades—colleges and universities appointed full-time development officers to manage ongoing fundraising programs and campaigns, reducing the need for the resident-manager model of consulting. Today even small colleges have a development or advancement staff of several people, and large research universities employ hundreds of professionals, led by a vice president for development or advancement who is a seasoned campaign manager. Professional associations, such as the Council for Advancement and Support of Education (CASE), offer extensive training programs in locations around the world. An increasing number of colleges and universities offer courses related to fundraising, and there are several prominent research centers dedicated to the study of philanthropy. Although bringing in a resident manager from a consulting firm to direct a campaign is now uncommon in higher education, consultants continue to play a role in ways that will be discussed later in this book.

The terms "fundraising," "development," and "advancement" are often used imprecisely and interchangeably today, although they have different definitions and historical origins. In its simplest definition, fundraising means soliciting gifts. Development is a broader concept that arose in higher education in the 1920s, and it reflected a shift in thinking. In this new approach, nurturing relationships with donors would become an ongoing process focused on the pursuit of the institution's long-term goals. It would be about not just fundraising but institutional *development*. Rather than engage in occasional capital campaigns directed by outside consultants, the ongoing process of cultivating relationships with donors would be managed by a full-time, campus-based *development officer*. With founding of the CASE in 1974, "institutional advancement," or just "advancement," was adopted as a broader umbrella designation, encompassing development as well as institutional communications and marketing, alumni relations, and on some campuses, other external relations functions.

From Capital to Comprehensive

Before the 1970s, most college and university campaigns were capital campaigns or, as Kent Dove calls them, "historical" capital campaigns, since the model is essentially obsolete in higher education now (Dove, 2000, p. 16). Like the campaigns that Ward and his contemporaries directed, they were special, intensive efforts, conducted about once or twice a decade, usually to raise funds for construction of a new campus building. The campaign generally consumed all of the institution's fundraising energies for a period of time (usually about three years) and included solicitation of its *entire constituency* for one-time commitments toward the featured project. (Most were not really one-time, since most institutions would undertake a capital campaign about once or twice a decade and would obviously return to some of the same people for another one-time commitment.)

Alumni annual giving funds were created in the nineteenth century and many had become ongoing programs by early in the twentieth. But, in the age of the capital campaign, the annual fund was often suspended for the duration of the campaign or was continued as a separate, low-key effort. All attention was focused on the campaign as the institution's highest priority, and all donors were asked to support it as theirs. Of course, there were a number of shortcomings to this model. First, donors might simply redirect their usual annual gift to the campaign, accomplishing little but to transfer money from one of the institution's pockets to another. The second problem was how to assure that individuals who had made multiyear pledges to the capital campaign would resume annual giving once their campaign pledges were completed. Restarting or rejuvenating the annual fund was often a significant challenge. And by suspending annual giving for the period of the campaign, the institution was not building its pipeline of younger donors who might become prospects for major gifts in a future campaign. The solution that emerged was to incorporate annual giving in the overall campaign and encourage donors to combine a capital gift and their annual giving into a single multiyear commitment. The campaign's goal then would reflect the total giving anticipated for both operating and capital purposes over the campaign period.

The 1970s also brought a new environment for what we now call planned giving. Some forms of planned giving, for example, bequests and gift annuities, appeared quite early in history and had always been among the largest sources of endowment gifts. But promotion of this type of giving by colleges and universities was fairly casual prior to passage of the Tax Reform Act of 1969. The 1969 legislation defined an array of giving vehicles, including charitable remainder trusts, charitable lead trusts, and pooled income funds. Along with various modifications enacted since, it still defines the ballpark for planned giving. Its passage opened up a new era in higher education fundraising that has seen increased marketing of planned giving by colleges and universities.

Beginning in about the 1970s, colleges and universities expanded the definition of the campaign to integrate capital, annual, and planned gifts under one umbrella—the comprehensive campaign. The trend toward this approach accelerated during the 1980s, 1990s, and 2000s, and indeed, almost all college or university campaigns today are comprehensive.

Like the capital campaign, a comprehensive campaign effort seeks support from the entire constituency of the institution. Rather than focusing the entire constituency on a single capital project or purpose, however, the market is differentiated and donors are solicited for support of campaign objectives coinciding with their interests and capabilities.

In addition to a more expansive definition of what gifts are included, the length of campaigns also increased over recent decades. The traditional capital campaign included about one to three years of active solicitation, with perhaps a three-to-five-year period allowed for the fulfillment of pledges. Since most campaigns were focused on a single building project, the payment of pledges in a relatively short time period was essential. Since the time at which the institution would receive control of a planned gift was unpredictable, such gifts were obviously not useful in support of such a project. By the 2000s, most comprehensive campaigns extended to seven years or longer, thus encompassing more annual giving and providing more time for the identification, cultivation, and solicitation of prospects for major and planned gifts to meet capital and endowment goals. (Today, CASE recommends that campaigns not exceed eight years, including the quiet and public phases, which are discussed in chapter 2.)

It is important to recognize that the comprehensive approach means that there is not likely to be a pot of available money to be allocated at its conclusion. The total raised includes annual gifts and program grants that already have been expended during the campaign period and commitments of future gifts that will be realized in later years. Clarity on this point is essential lest unrealistic expectations of a windfall be raised by communication of the campaign's success. For that reason, recommended best practice is to establish separate goals for current and deferred gifts at the outset of the campaign and to keep them distinct in reporting campaign progress (CASE, 2009, p. 84).

Institutions still also conduct single-purpose or focused campaigns from time to time. As the term suggests, such campaigns are undertaken to accomplish some specific purpose or project, for example, construction of a new building, endowment of professorships or scholarships, or development of a new school or institute. They are different from the traditional capital campaign because solicitations are limited to a subset of the institution's constituency that has a particular interest in that project, for example, alumni of an individual school or program. And they are not comprehensive campaigns because they do not include institution-wide priorities or, usually, annual giving.

CAMPAIGN FUNDAMENTAL PRINCIPLES

The most often quoted definition of a campaign is that offered by Kent Dove in his classic 2000 book on the subject: "an organized, intensive fundraising effort . . . to secure extraordinary gifts and pledges . . . for a specific purpose or programs . . . during a specified period of time" (p. 5). But it is worth unpacking the definition to understand the fundamental principles of campaigns, all of which reflect some implicit assumptions about human nature and society.

1. A campaign has an *announced* goal and deadline.

As we have seen many times in crises and disasters, people respond to urgency and perform best under pressure, when the price of failure would be high. It is human nature—and perhaps characteristically American—to defer action until the need for it is clear and immediate. Generations of students have written their papers the night before they are due, and there are lines at the post office on April 15 (as well as slowing of the Internet as electronic filers log on just before midnight). Goals and deadlines motivate intensive and exceptional effort.

The financial needs of higher education institutions, while important, are usually related to long-term goals and are justified intellectually. While many people hold deep feelings for colleges and universities, their financial needs do not necessarily inspire the same emotion as true emergencies. For example, providing scholarships so that young people have educational opportunities and can become leaders in society is a goal of critical importance to the future. But it is simply not as compelling as the scenes of starving children or homeless storm victims on CNN. Colleges and universities may present opportunities for philanthropy, but they are not usually viewed as objects of charity.

Nor does fundraising for higher education have the same natural urgency of a political campaign. Following the fundraising success of Barack Obama's presidential campaign in 2008, especially its innovative use of the Internet to raise funds from millions of small donors, there has been considerable discussion about how similar techniques may be applied in higher education fundraising. Indeed, the Internet is becoming an ever more important tool, especially for alumni relations and communications and in the annual fund. But there are also big differences between political and philanthropic fundraising. For one, since political campaigns end on Election Day, there is a built-in deadline that is not inherent in fundraising for institutions that expect to exist in perpetuity.

For a college or university, announcing a campaign goal and a deadline for its achievement raises the stakes. The reputation of the institution and its leaders is on the line. An exciting challenge and the risk of failure help to motivate action, create excitement, and gain visibility—both for the campaign itself and for the substantive academic vision that it is intended to advance. Placing the institution's academic goals and related financial needs in the spotlight also reveals the magnitude of the overall effort and puts it in context, providing potential donors with a standard of appropriate response.

A fundraising effort that has no goal—for example, that is intended to "raise as much as we can" or that continues until a certain total has been achieved—is not a campaign. It is perhaps a program. A goal and deadline that are known only to those within the institution may be motivating to them, but they do not necessarily influence the thinking of those from whom support is sought. That is more like a sales initiative than a campaign. A campaign has a specific dollar goal and a deadline for achieving it that are announced to the public, in order to capture attention and motivate timely action by all whose participation is essential to its success.

2. A campaign is focused on obtaining support for *specific* purposes that address strategic priorities of the institution.

People give money to meet important needs or pursue exciting opportunities, not merely because they are asked to do so. Just "give"—or even "please give"—is not a very compelling request absent substantive reasons to do so.

People respond to objectives that are concrete and not so much to generalities. They respond to lofty ideals, but also need to see the connection between the specific actions they are asked to take and how those ideals will be advanced. Campaign priorities may be broadly defined, but they are determined up front as a part of the institution's overall strategic and campaign planning. Campaign goals are justified on the basis of how their achievement will advance the college or university toward its stated vision of the future. Campaign gifts are solicited toward specific objectives related to that vision. In other words, campaigns are undertaken to *advance* the college or university, not just to raise money.

3. A campaign employs rated prospect lists and specific asks.

Wealth and income are unevenly distributed, in American society and virtually every society that has ever existed. Most people know where they stand in the economic hierarchy and also have an innate sense of fairness—a desire to do their fair share but also the expectation that others will do theirs as well. Despite its Marxist overtones, the idea of "from each according to his or her ability" is one with which most people agree with regard to giving.

Recognizing this social reality, campaign fundraising is based on the principle of proportional giving. In other words, individuals are asked to give in proportion to their capacity to do so. But they are not asked simply to give what they can. That would not be a campaign, but rather a collection. In a campaign, the top prospects are asked for specific *amounts* for specific *purposes*, based on an assessment of their financial capabilities and interests.

A common misunderstanding is to think that fundraising can be undertaken according to the multiplication table, for example, that $1 million can be raised by soliciting $1,000 each from one thousand people. That almost always fails because it does not reflect the reality of disproportional financial ability and the natural tendency of human beings—even if equally committed to the cause—to determine their fair share according to their perceptions of their relative economic standing in whatever community may be relevant. Preparing for a campaign includes identifying prospects for major gifts and rating them with regard to their financial capacity, which in part determines the order in which they will be solicited.

4. A campaign follows the principle of sequential fundraising.

Again, most people want to do what is fair and what is expected of them. And they tend to look to the behavior of others to determine what that means. Accordingly, a campaign follows a careful process that starts with the solicitation of those deemed capable of the largest commitments and those who are closest to the institution—those who are seen as having the greatest stake in the campaign's success. This approach is sometimes described as solicitation "from top down and the inside out" and is generally known as "sequential fundraising," a term attributed to the legendary campaign consultant George Brakeley Jr. (McGoldrick and Robell, 2002, p. 141).

Following this principle, among the first people solicited are members of the institution's governing board (and/or the board of its affiliated foundation) and the most highly capable and committed gift prospects. Following the inside-out principle, the faculty and staff are often solicited early in the campaign. They may not be top prospects in terms of their financial capacity, but they are clearly among the closest members of the campus family. The top-down/inside-out process unfolds over the course of the campaign, and discipline in following it is important to maximize support.

A fundraising effort that begins with a solicitation of the institution's entire constituency is not a campaign. It is an appeal. It is unlikely to maximize giving because it does not provide those who are asked with any standards or visible role models by which to judge what their own response should be.

There is a high risk in not following the sequence or not executing the process effectively. Early failures or mistakes may doom the entire effort or end it prematurely. For example, a development colleague once called me for advice on a very difficult situation in which a campaign chair, who was also a wealthy trustee and top donor prospect, had been enlisted without a clear understanding of what would be required. The president had asked him to chair the campaign, and he accepted. Other trustees were told of his decision. But he then told the president he would be unable to make more than a token gift at the outset of the campaign. He explained that he had made significant commitments to other institutions and that he was obligated to complete those over the next few years. Having suffered a decline in his wealth as a result of the stock market, he explained, he was unable to consider another major commitment right now. "I will make a small gift now and consider a significant gift later on in the campaign," he said, "but in the meantime I will help you with raising major gifts from others who may be in a better position than I am." As my development colleague understood, this was a fiasco situation. The president had made a critical mistake in enlisting this chair, and the chair had accepted without understanding the implications of his situation. He would be unable to solicit any gift more than the token one he was prepared to make, and questions about his commitment would dog any subsequent campaign efforts.

The top prospects and campaign insiders have the opportunity to leverage the impact of their gifts through their influence on the giving of those further down the hierarchy, or to jeopardize the entire effort with an inadequate or untimely response. My advice to my development colleague, and to his president, was to have a frank conversation with the chair. The result of that conversation needed to be some (perhaps creative) plan through which the chair could make an appropriate commitment to the campaign now, or some graceful approach to bringing in new campaign leadership.

Consistent with the principle of sequential fundraising, campaigns are conducted in phases, in order to assure appropriate attention to top prospects and insiders before the campaign is rolled out to the broader constituency. Rolling out the campaign prematurely runs the risk of preemptive gifts that lower the standards for the duration. It often takes presidential leadership and resolve to maintain the discipline.

5. A campaign engages organized volunteer leadership.

People support institutions and causes with which they are involved. And people follow the example of others whom they admire and respect. They wish to be associated with others who are viewed as successful and worthy individuals and not with those whose reputations do not impress them. They tend to discount assertions by those with obvious self-interest and to seek reassurance in the endorsement of others who have no personal stake in the matter. That is why people are selective about who they accept as a friend on social networking sites and why political candidates seek the endorsements of others who are well regarded within their communities or parties. That is why consumers give greater credibility to the reviews of fellow consumers than to the representations of advertising or salespersons. These tendencies of human nature with regard to fundraising and giving are supported by academic research as well as practitioner experience (Lindahl, 2010, pp. 85–105).

A campaign is led by prominent volunteers, whose own prestige and credibility authenticate the institution and its goals. Their visible involvement makes a statement about the importance of the college or university and the worthiness of its campaign. They make it attractive for others who are like them, or who aspire to be, to participate with them in the campaign, through giving and in other ways. And, of course, they may have access to and influence with others who may evade the attention of the president, dean, or development officer.

Of course, in reality, many campaign gifts are solicited by the president, other academic officers, and development or advancement staff members. Indeed, many campaigns today are primarily staff driven, especially at research universities with large development offices. The number of solicitations required to achieve a big campaign goal and the complexity of some gift arrangements simply dictate that professionals play a substantial role. Most presidents are actively engaged in cultivating donors and soliciting gifts, often accompanied by their chief development officers. In some cases, volunteers may be the leaders of the campaign primarily in name. But such titular leadership is not the most desirable situation.

College and university presidencies are positions that command great prestige and respect. In most cases, senior development officers, especially vice presidents, are also viewed as significant figures in their institutions. But the legitimacy of a solicitation is increased when it is issued, or at least endorsed, by volunteer leaders who are motivated only by their commitment to an institution or a cause, especially if they have demonstrated the sincerity of that commitment through their own significant gifts. Their involvement and example may change the solicitation from a transaction to an invitation.

Volunteer leaders accept shared responsibility for the campaign's success. This shared responsibility calls forth their own giving and drives their participation in the cultivation and solicitation of other donors. Sharing responsibility for the campaign is thus essential to maximize the institution's reach into its constituency and also, to be quite frank, to minimize finger pointing should there be disappointments or setbacks as the campaign unfolds.

Campaign volunteer leadership is organized in a structure, usually including a chair or co-chairs, a campaign steering committee, and perhaps chairs of committees focused on various academic units, donor constituencies, or particular campaign objectives. Some alternative structures are discussed in chapter 3 of this book.

6. A campaign emphasizes major gifts.

Although most campaigns today are comprehensive, they emphasize the principal and major gifts that will comprise the largest portion of funds raised toward the campaign's capital and endowment objectives. In past decades it was common to speak of the 80/20 rule, that is, the fact that about 80 percent of the campaign's total would result from about 20 percent of gifts. In the 1990s and 2000s, most campaigns were demonstrating that the rule had moved to something more like 90/10, with almost 90 percent of the total raised resulting from just 10 percent of gifts to the campaign. Some question whether the latter pattern will continue amidst predictions of slower economic growth in the future. It is a question to which this book will return in a later section.

Another historical fundraising axiom is the "Rule of Thirds," attributable to Harold J. Seymour (1966). It held that about one-third of the campaign total would come from the top ten gifts, a second third would come from the next one hundred gifts, and the final third of the total would come from all the smaller gifts below that. But in the boom times of the late 1990s and mid-2000s, many campaigns were showing much more concentrated results, with more than half of the goal resulting from just a handful of the largest gifts. This point will be explored further in chapter 4.

Campaigns are undertaken to raise the sights of donors across the board, but especially to secure the principal and major gifts that can have a significant, even transformational, impact on the institution and its programs.

CAMPAIGNS TODAY

Changes in higher education and the economy during the 1990s and the 2000s further increased the prevalence and magnitude of comprehensive campaigns. Even before the onset of recession in 2007, many colleges and universities were facing significant financial challenges. State budgets were under pressure, as other public needs increasingly competed with higher education for appropriated funds. Rising tuition levels over recent decades in both private and public institutions, the growing burden of student debt, and the increased sensitivity of families to college costs were defining a limit to the revenue that could be anticipated from student fees. Demographic trends suggested that many colleges would face rising competition for students in the years ahead, increasing the importance of marketing and branding and bringing new appreciation for the visibility and communication opportunities that a campaign provides.

The financial goals of campaigns have grown steadily and impressively over more than a century, despite the ups and downs of economic cycles. Harvard's campaign in 1904–1905 raised $2.5 million for faculty salaries. Its next campaign, in 1919–1920 raised $14 million for the Harvard endowment. By the late 1950s, Harvard raised what historian Scott Cutlip (1965, p. 480) calls "the staggering sum of $82,775,553." Stanford broke the $1 billion barrier with a campaign launched in 1987 and, in 1999, Harvard became the first to exceed the $2 billion mark, raising $2.3 billion in a five-year campaign.

The early 2000s brought the dot-com bust, 9/11, and an economic recession, but by the middle of the decade the markets had recovered and institutions were launching campaigns with even more ambitious goals. Columbia University began the quiet phase of a $4 billion campaign in 2004 and made a public announcement in 2006 with $1.6 billion already committed (Strout, 2006a). Columbia's goal was exceeded one month later with Stanford University's announcement of a $4.3 billion campaign, the largest in the history of higher education to that time (Strout, 2006b). Near the end of 2007, the *Chronicle of Higher Education* reported more than thirty-one institutions engaged in campaigns with goals of $1 billion or more, including eleven public institutions (Breslow, 2007). The onset of recession in December 2007 complicated both campaigns that were already under way and those that were in planning. But, as in investing, in fundraising it is helpful to maintain a long-term perspective.

One of the most prominent trends of recent decades has been the growth of fundraising by public colleges and universities. Once mostly reliant on state appropriations, public universities now compete with private institutions for philanthropy to replace declining state support and to secure capital to advance their goals. UCLA set a record by raising $3.05 billion in a ten-year campaign that concluded in 2006. In the same year, the University of Virginia announced a $3 billion goal, with $950 million already having been committed during the campaign's silent phase (Strout, 2006a). In September 2008, despite a weak national economy, the University of California–Berkeley went public with a $3 billion campaign. Over $1.3 billion already had been committed to the campaign, which was scheduled to run until 2013 (University of California–Berkeley, 2008).

While multimillion dollar and multibillion dollar campaigns at research universities draw the greatest media attention, campaigns have become the norm at most higher education institutions. CASE's 2007 *Campaign Report* identified 171 campaigns that were currently under way at research/doctoral, master's, and bachelor's institutions, as well as two-year community colleges and independent schools. Goals ranged from $1 million to $4 billion, with a median of $50 million. Most campaigns were comprehensive in nature, with 31 percent of the total goals for capital projects, 37 percent for endowment, and 32 percent for current operations. Community college campaigns were somewhat different from those of other types of institutions, with two-thirds of their goals for capital projects (CASE, 2007, p. 4). CASE's report demonstrates that campaigns have become a key advancement strategy for institutions of all sizes and categories.

Campaigns also have become common at colleges and universities around the world. CASE opened a European office in London in 1994 and an Asia-Pacific office in Singapore in 2007. By 2008, its membership had grown to include institutions in sixty countries. In 2004, the University of Cambridge launched a campaign for £1 billion to mark its eight hundredth anniversary—a milestone rather astonishing to an American! The University of Oxford announced its £1.25 billion campaign in 2008, with £575 million already having been committed toward its goal.

CAMPAIGN PROS AND CONS

Launching a campaign offers unique benefits and opportunities. But there are some who question whether it is a universally effective strategy or whether, indeed, it is a twentieth-century idea that has outlived its time. Among the benefits of a campaign are the following:

- Preparing for a campaign may bring focus to the discussion of an institution's future and discipline to its planning.

- The campaign generates visibility and excitement and engages all of the institution's constituencies.
- The visibility of the campaign provides opportunities to also advance important institutional goals for communication, marketing, alumni relations, and branding.
- The campaign process leverages the leadership gifts of the most committed donors to raise the sights of others.
- A campaign enables the governing board, and/or the board of an affiliated foundation, to fulfill its responsibilities by helping to assure the institution's financial future and to gain the satisfaction of participating in its advancement.
- A campaign is likely to have a lasting impact on giving, resulting in higher levels of ongoing annual and capital support in the years following its completion.

This effect is illustrated in figure 1.1, based on the work of John Cash, a senior consultant with the consulting firm of Marts & Lundy. The lower line depicts the trend of gift revenue and the trajectory it would be expected to follow if ongoing fundraising programs were continued absent a campaign. As the upper line shows, gift revenue increases substantially in response to the campaign, as gifts are made and pledges are paid, providing a campaign premium over what otherwise would have been raised. Gift revenue declines at the conclusion of the campaign, as pledges are fulfilled, and then it resumes growth at roughly its pre-campaign rate. But it typically does not return to its pre-campaign level, producing important post-campaign value in the form of permanently higher annual and capital support. In other

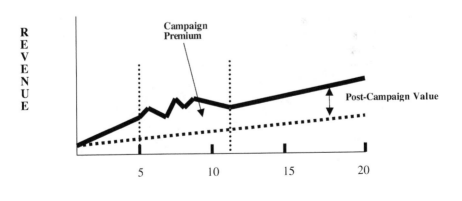

YEARS

Figure 1.1. Post-Campaign Value. SOURCE: Adapted from Cash, John M., "Presentation to the San Jose State University Academic Senate," January 29, 2007. http://www.sjsu.edu/senate/Najjarcc.pdf, accessed January 26, 2009.

words, to use the common phrase, a campaign can help take the institution to "the next level" in terms of long-term philanthropic revenue.

However, some suggest that the comprehensive campaign may have outlived its usefulness and is not a model well suited to patterns of wealth, attitudes of donors, or the realities of higher education today. Their reasoning often runs along the following lines.

The campaign model reflects obsolete assumptions about giving. Many corporations and foundations are no longer responsive to campaigns and follow the concept of strategic philanthropy, supporting causes and organizations that align with their own goals and priorities. Individual donors are becoming more like corporations and foundations in their thinking, also taking a strategic or entrepreneurial approach and preferring to support programs with measurable short-term impact rather than the traditional campaign priorities of annual giving, endowment, and bricks-and-mortar projects.

Individuals' readiness to give often is dependent on their own circumstances rather than the institution's timetable. Older donors will consider major gifts in connection with their retirement or estate planning, that is, when they have reached the dispositive phase of their lives. Younger donors may give when they sell a business or receive a bonus, the timing of which is, again, related to their own circumstances rather than the timetable of the campaign. Trying to force philanthropy into the deadlines and defined priorities of a campaign may result in less eventual support than nurturing relationships over time, guiding donors to discern their interests and values, and asking for a gift when the time is right for them and a purpose of mutual interest has emerged. In other words, some argue, a continuous major gifts program is a strategy better suited to today's realities than is a campaign.

Some observe that circumstances on the institution's side are also fluid. Over the course of a seven-year or longer campaign, institutional priorities may change. New programs and units may emerge on campus. Deans and other campus leaders, including presidents, may depart and new ones arrive, bringing different agendas. Changing economic conditions may alter the relative importance of endowment and annual giving or the priority attached to scholarships, technology, or research. New opportunities for expansion or growth may emerge that were not anticipated when the campaign's priorities were identified. Campaign priorities set for almost a decade may either be insufficiently flexible to accommodate such changes or may be so broad as to be uninspiring. In the latter situation, the campaign may become all about the bottom line, and the institution may be inclined to accept gifts for purposes that do not meet its essential needs or that may even lead it off in directions that are not prudent or consistent with its mission. The campaign may achieve its dollar goals, but campaign gifts may be neither transformational nor useful.

Finally, some might say, the campaign model, developed in fundraising for community-based nonprofit organizations more than a century ago, simply does not reflect the society in which we live today. Traditional concepts about communities, on which the ideas of proportional giving, sequential fundraising, and other campaign principles are based, no longer apply in our mobile, global, and socially networked society.

The preceding are all worthy observations, and a campaign may not be the best strategy for every institution at all times. But the campaign model also has evolved to address some of the changing realities that its critics mention. Longer campaigns provide the opportunity to cultivate relationships with prospects and to track their readiness to give within the time frame of the campaign. The comprehensive definition of campaigns may accommodate the situations of some planned gift donors, includes specific projects that may attract entrepreneurial donors, and encompasses annual giving, which may provide a gateway for younger donors. And frequent campaigns essentially produce an environment of continuous fundraising that may capture the interest of donors as they evolve along their own timetables.

Moreover, today's campaigns are more than intensive fundraising efforts. They are integrated efforts to advance colleges and universities with additional resources as well as increased visibility and understanding of their missions. Campaign communications help to *build communities* by highlighting important purposes and goals, rooted in common values, and by providing volunteers and donors with the satisfaction of helping to share in their achievement.

At the most basic level, a campaign changes the conversation. Rather than "We would like to come and talk with you about a gift," the campaign discussion begins with "We would like to come and talk with you about the future of the college." The campaign provides the rationale and the framework for conversations that may produce resources now as well as raise awareness and deepen understanding and relationships of long-term importance to the institution, in various ways.

THE PRESIDENT'S CAMPAIGN LEADERSHIP

As stated at the beginning of this chapter, leading a campaign is an expectation for most college and university president today—at institutions large and small, public and private. The campaign's priorities and objectives are often the embodiment of the president's agenda for his or her time in office. Successful completion of the campaign is an important measure in defining a successful presidency and a great opportunity to advance the college or university on a president's watch. But the campaign also comes with risk and cost for the president, both professionally and personally.

Campaigns bring political risk. Preparing for a campaign requires setting priorities and making them visible. That inevitably generates on-campus debate, as certain programs, units, or projects are identified as more important than others while the aspirations and expectations of others are deferred or denied. At the least, the pride of some campus programs may be wounded, as their priorities are not sufficiently evident in the campaign.

Engaging volunteer leaders, including trustees and others, in planning and implementation of a campaign is sure to heighten their awareness and give rise to their opinions about priorities, perhaps involving them more deeply in academic decision making than some would view as desirable.

Because volunteer leaders share responsibility for the campaign, and attach their own pride and reputation to its success, they will be highly attuned to the fundraising effort and performance of the president, deans, development officers, and other campus leaders. They may not hesitate to express their views if they find the campaign lacking in some way.

Although there are notable and a growing number of exceptions, most presidents have risen to their office through academic careers. Having chosen teaching and scholarship as pursuits well suited to their talents and temperaments, the presidency draws them in other directions. Of course, that has long been the case, as the financial, management, and legal challenges facing college and university executives have increasingly crowded out time for reflection or the full enjoyment of relationships with campus colleagues. But engaging in a campaign pulls a president even farther from his or her natural roots. The campaign may occupy much of the president's time, require extensive travel, and fill late nights with meetings and social events. A campaign may require that the president spend more time off campus than on campus and interact more with business leaders than with professors or students. That presents a subtle but real risk that a president may lose touch with the culture and core values of the institution that he or she leads and experience what one author describes as "the transition from the life of the mind to the life of the wallet" (Wilson, 2007). If that occurs, it is likely to diminish both the president's personal happiness and his or her professional effectiveness.

Campaigning presidents need to anticipate and address both the political and personal risks of engagement in a campaign. Some of the former may be mitigated by acquiring a full understanding of the campaign process and the strategic options that it presents, as well as the careful selection of campaign staff, sound planning, and adherence to principles explored in this book. The latter may require setting some limits and making hard choices.

For example, when Neil Rudenstine was president of Harvard he created a "private time-distribution formula" to assure that he would devote at least one-half of his time to academic matters and no more than one-third to fundraising, assuring that he would stay in touch with the intellectual life of the institution (Wilson, 2007). But many presidents may find it difficult to adhere to such discipline amidst the pressure of campaign goals and deadlines, the demands of their chief development officers, and the expectations of campaign leaders, trustees, and donors.

The next chapter summarizes the basic phases of a campaign with an emphasis on the key decisions and tasks that each requires. Subsequent chapters discuss campaign leadership, planning, and implementation in greater detail.

REFERENCES

American Council on Education. (2008). "American College President." www .acenet.edu/Content/NavigationMenu/ProgramsServices/CPA/Executive _Summary.htm (accessed November 10, 2008).

Breslow, Jason M. (2007). "Updates on Billion-Dollar Campaigns at 31 Universities" [electronic version]. *Chronicle of Higher Education*, December 3. chronicle .com/daily/2007/12/851n.htm (accessed November 19, 2008).

Council for Advancement and Support of Education (CASE). (2007). *CASE Campaign Report*. Washington, DC: Author.

———. (2009). *CASE Reporting Standards and Management Guidelines*. 4th edition. Washington, DC: Author.

Cutlip, Scott M. (1965). *Fund Raising in the United States: Its Role in American Philanthropy*. New Brunswick, NJ: Rutgers University Press.

Dove, Kent E. (2000). *Conducting a Successful Capital Campaign*. 2nd edition. San Francisco: Jossey-Bass.

Lindahl, Wesley E. (2010). *Principles of Fundraising: Theory and Practice*. Sudbury, MA: Jones and Bartlett Publishers.

Masterson, Kathryn. (2009). "Want to Be a College President? Search Consultants Share How-To's" [electronic version]. *Chronicle of Higher Education*, June 9. chronicle.com/daily/2009/06/19652n.htm?utm_source=at&utm_medium=en (accessed June 9, 2009).

McGoldrick, William P., and Paul A. Robell. (2002). "Campaigning in the New Century." In Michael J. Worth (Ed.), *New Strategies for Educational Fund Raising*. Westport, CT: American Council on Education and Praeger, pp. 135–152.

Seymour, Harold J. (1966). *Designs for Fund Raising*. New York: McGraw-Hill.

Strout, Erin. (2006a). "Columbia U. Kicks Off $4-Billion Campaign." *Chronicle of Higher Education* 53, no. 8 (October 13), p. A38.

———. (2006b). "Stanford Announces Biggest Campaign." *Chronicle of Higher Education* 53, no. 9 (October 20), p. A35.

University of California–Berkeley. (2008). "UC Berkeley Launches Major Multi-Year Campaign to Raise $3 Billion." Press release, September 19, 2008. www.berkeley

.edu/news/media/releases/2008/09/19_campaign.shtml (accessed November 10, 2008).

Wilson, Charles. (2007). "Degree Requirements in Fund-Raising" [electronic version]. *New York Times Magazine*, September 30. www.nytimes.com/2007/09/30/magazine/30wwln-charticle-wilson-t.html?fta=y (accessed April 22, 2009).

2

Campaign Phases:
Key Decisions and Tasks

A campaign unfolds in phases, and discipline in following the sequence is important to success. A critical error, especially in the early phases, may doom the entire effort to failure, just as a poorly laid foundation can cause a building to collapse. This chapter provides an overview of the phases of a typical campaign and summarizes the key decisions and tasks that need to be completed in each phase, with an emphasis on the leadership role of the president.

The balance of this book is organized according to the phases outlined here. Following a discussion of the campaign team in chapter 3, chapters 4 and 5 go into detail on Phase I (planning the campaign), and chapter 6 discusses Phases II, III, IV, and V (executing the campaign). Chapter 7 focuses on the art of cultivating donor relationships and soliciting campaign gifts. Chapter 8 then considers Phase VI (post-campaign evaluation, planning, and stewardship). Campaign communications and events permeate all phases and are mentioned as appropriate along the way, but chapter 9 discusses some key points related to that topic.

Different authors describe the phases of a campaign in different ways, using a somewhat varied vocabulary. But the essence of the model is always the same and follows the time-tested principles of campaigning discussed in chapter 1. Figure 2.1 illustrates the key phases of the campaign as described in this chapter:

- Phase I: Planning
- Phase II: Quiet phase (also called quiet period, silent phase, advance gifts phase, nucleus fund phase)
- Phase III: Kickoff

- Phase IV: Public phase
- Phase V: Closing phase (including the victory celebration)
- Phase VI: Post-campaign evaluation, planning, and stewardship

As figure 2.1 suggests, the phases overlap. For example, there is not always a neat boundary between what is institutional planning, whether called strategic planning or something else, and what is campaign planning. A campaign plan should be completed and approved by the governing board before the campaign quiet phase begins, but planning does not end with the beginning of solicitation or after the campaign kickoff. Plans need to be adjusted throughout the campaign as experience and conditions dictate. While the quiet phase of the campaign is focused on the solicitation of advance leadership gifts—toward the campaign's nucleus fund—that is not to suggest that the cultivation and solicitation of high-rated prospects come to an end with the kickoff and the beginning of the public phase of the campaign. The closing phase is really a component of the public phase, so they are depicted as overlapping.

Of course, no one size fits all. As architects say, form should follow function. An individual college or university may need to adapt this basic model to fit its own particular circumstances. And changes in wealth, society, and communication may make it necessary to refine the model to fit new realities in the decades ahead. But, again, the basic model reflects fundamental principles of human nature and psychology that are relatively unchanging. Too much creativity in diverging from the process may result in failure of the campaign or—at the least—a result that is less than might otherwise have been attained.

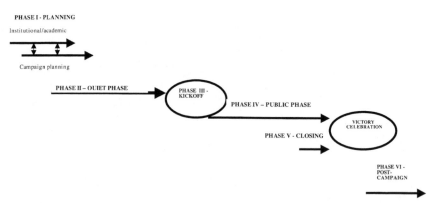

Figure 2.1.   Phases of the Campaign

PHASE I: PLANNING

Preparation for a campaign begins with planning at two levels. The institution needs to engage in planning to establish its academic directions, priorities, and substantive goals for the future and identify the financial resources necessary to achieving them. At the same time, the development office or the foundation will be planning with a more specific focus on the steps necessary to attain campaign readiness. As figure 2.1 suggests, these two processes are concurrent, interactive, and iterative. The academic goals identified through institutional planning shape the campaign priorities and objectives, while realistic assessments of the potential for fundraising need to be reflected in the institutional plan. For example, some institutional priorities may be found to be attractive to donors and can be funded through the campaign, while others may require alternative approaches.

The campaign should not drive institutional planning; rather, a comprehensive strategy for advancing the college or university should include a campaign as *one* important vehicle for accomplishing the institution's vision of its future. However, it is only realistic to acknowledge that in some cases anticipation of a campaign energizes institutional planning.

Academic Planning

The most successful campaigns are those that are rooted in the institution's well-considered academic directions and goals—and big, integrating ideas—rather than a disconnected wish list of gift opportunities assembled by the development office. An anecdote recounted in the *Chronicle of Higher Education* illustrates the point. One university solicited a prospect, who also had been a previous donor, for a $25 million gift to complete its multimillion-dollar campaign. The individual refused, but shortly afterward gave $50 million to another institution for its medical school. When the first university asked why, he responded, "You asked me to help finish a campaign. They asked me to help cure cancer" (Strout, 2007a, p. A21). Substantive purposes can translate into a strong case for support, but a dollar goal by itself is hollow. Effective fundraising is undertaken as a means to accomplishing important change, not as an end in itself.

The process for institutional planning is among the first critical decisions the president needs to make. There are, of course, various opinions about how institutions should go about this activity.

Strategic planning, in higher education as well as business, has its fans as well as critics. Management professor Henry Mintzberg became a leading voice among the critics with his widely cited 1994 book *The Rise and Fall of Strategic Planning*, in which he argues that the strategic planning process overly emphasizes rational analysis and that its lockstep process does not invite creativity or synthesis; indeed, that it too often leads to a cumbersome document that does not include an actual strategy for the organization (cited in Chait, Ryan, and Taylor, 2005, pp. 56–57).

In their 2005 book *Governance as Leadership*, Richard Chait, William Ryan, and Barbara Taylor take further aim at strategic planning and write that "disillusionment with strategic planning has escalated." They observe that in too many plans, "dreams trump reality," that is, they include "blue sky" goals without addressing existing barriers to their achievement. Too many include specific goals but no more than a vague strategy for achieving them. When a strategy is described, it too often fails to acknowledge the implications for change in the status quo of organizational architecture, people, and resources. They call this "planning by wishful thinking" (p. 58).

According to Chait and his colleagues, formal plans often reflect overconfidence in predictions about the future and do not adequately anticipate unforeseen circumstances. And, finally, they observe that some strategic plans really reflect the consensus of the CEO and senior executives, which the board is asked to merely ratify. They write,

> At that juncture . . . [when the strategic plan is presented to the board] . . . trustees are invited . . . to provide assistance, as needed and requested by management, to *implement* a strategy predicated on the ideas of others. Cognizant of these patterns, some trustees begin to wonder why disenfranchisement starts at the top of the organization chart, and CEOs start to wonder why trustee disengagement seems to accelerate after ratification of the plan. (Chait et al., 2005, p. 59)

Chait and his coauthors do not specifically address the circumstance of preparing for a campaign. But if their observation about the board's noninvolvement in planning is generally correct, that has implications for campaigns. A campaign based on plans in which the board feels no ownership may be one that trustees do not feel strongly compelled to lead or support.

The fundraising consulting firm Marts & Lundy conducted a study of higher education institutions that had engaged in strategic planning prior to a campaign and others that had not. The study report's author concluded that strategic planning brought important advantages, indeed that "strategic planning is an investment in the outcome of the campaign" (Thomsen, 2009, p. 5).

The study participants were presidents, vice presidents for development, and directors of development who had recently completed campaigns. Of the 104 institutions included in the study, 57 percent had conducted strategic planning and 47 percent had not, but *all* of the respondents—including those who had not planned—said they would recommend strategic planning in advance of a campaign. Most of those who had not engaged in strategic planning nevertheless reached their campaign goals, but reported their belief that they did not fully capitalize on opportunities. Study participants' comments suggested that without strategic planning, "donors were not as engaged; on-campus ownership of the campaign was not galvanized and therefore not as passionately shared with external constituents; and there was a lack of clarity on how the campaign was interlinked with the mission and vision [of the institution]" (Thomsen, 2009, p. 6).

Those institutions that had engaged in strategic planning took a variety of approaches, including 79 percent that engaged in an institution-wide strategic plan (Thomsen, 2009, p. 9). While some presidents noted the difficulty in bringing an entire campus together in a strategic plan, many cited advantages. Strategic planning developed a strong sense of ownership internally; helped interrelate the plan and key messages; shaped the case statement; and increased understanding of campaign priorities among external constituents who participated in the planning process. Planning also served to build a culture of philanthropy; improve understanding between the chief development officer and the chief financial officer; and break down silos between academic units (Thomsen, 2009, pp. 9–11).

Again, this book does not recommend any particular model for institutional planning, but from the campaign perspective, an inclusive approach offers the advantages mentioned above. A plan that is just delivered—by the president, the chief development officer, or someone else—may be exactly right, even brilliant. But it may belong only to the hearts of its authors and not engender the broad ownership, commitment, and support that a successful campaign requires.

Campaign Planning

At the same time as institutional planning is under way, campaign planning and preparation also takes place. This includes assessing the pool of donor prospects and intensifying prospect research and evaluation; hiring and training the professional staff needed to manage the campaign; preparing a campaign budget; identifying and involving potential volunteer leaders of the campaign; intensifying communication with and cultivation of leadership gift prospects; setting campaign policies; drafting a case statement; writing a campaign plan; and perhaps undertaking a market test or feasibility study. The preliminary goal of the campaign and its objectives may be revised to reflect insight gained from the market test. That creates another feedback loop into institutional planning as well as the need for refinements to the list of campaign priorities, the case statement, and the campaign plan.

The campaign plan is a written document that may be of varied length, but consistent with CASE's (Council for Advancement and Support of Education) campaign management guidelines, it should at least describe

- the institution's needs that will be addressed;
- the campaign reporting policies to which the institution will adhere, including the treatment of outright gifts and pledges, irrevocable deferred gifts, and gifts-in-kind;
- the manner of considering and acting upon exceptions to those policies;
- the tentative goal for both featured objectives (usually endowment or construction) and other objectives (usually expendable programmatic support and annual fund revenues);
- an objective analysis of the fundraising potential of the institution;
- the purpose and duration of the quiet or nucleus phase of the campaign;
- the duration of the public phase of the campaign. (CASE, 2009, pp. 82–83)

Chapters 4 and 5 of this book provide a more detailed discussion of the actions and decisions required in campaign planning.

The discussion in chapter 1 acknowledged that undertaking a campaign does present some risks, for the institution and its president. But the process also includes some checks and balances to minimize the chance of failure. First, if a market test or feasibility study has been completed, there is an opportunity at that point to revise the campaign's working goal and objectives to assure that they are consistent with reality and not the product of wild optimism—or unwarranted caution. A second checkpoint comes after the completion of Phase II, when the rubber has really hit the road with solicitation of advance gifts from the institution's top prospects toward the nucleus fund. If the quiet phase goes well, announcement of the goal then can proceed as planned or, perhaps, the goal may even be increased with some confidence. If the key early solicitations turn out to be disappointing, or if some campaign priorities attract more or less support than was anticipated, that provides yet another opportunity to make revisions before the campaign is announced and the institution's reputation and its president's credibility are placed on the line. Should economic conditions turn unfavorable, the quiet phase may be extended so that the campaign announcement will be accompanied with a sufficient nucleus fund to build confidence and give credibility to the ultimate goal.

The transition from Phase I to Phase II is often a point that brings some risk, and there may be a need for presidential leadership in insisting on adherence to the campaign process and the plan. Many people, including faculty, deans, members of the governing board, and other volunteer leaders, may have been involved in planning and discussion about the campaign for perhaps one to two years. Some may be eager to just get on with it and announce the campaign. But announcing the campaign prematurely violates the principle of sequential fundraising. It reduces the incentive for advance gift donors to make a maximum commitment. It detracts from the drama of the formal announcement. And it introduces the probability of preemptive gifts that are far below the capacity of those who make them.

The situation is analogous to the early phases of a political campaign. The candidate's intention to run is widely assumed and implied by his or her behavior. But the candidate maintains some coyness about his or her intentions and a formal announcement is delayed, in order to build momentum, maintain interest, and continue testing the waters before plunging in. That process also preserves the opportunity for the candidate to pull back from a formal announcement should the polls become discouraging. In a college or university campaign, the preannouncement period similarly calls for managing expectations and, again, the president may need to be the one to insist on discipline.

PHASE II: QUIET PHASE

As discussed in chapter 1, campaign solicitations begin from the top down, and the inside out. While the campaign is still in its quiet phase, that is, before its goal has been formally announced, advance gifts are solicited from the top prospects and those who are the most inside of insiders, including the governing board of the college or university and, at public institutions, its affiliated foundation. These advance gifts comprise the nucleus fund, the total of commitments that will be announced at the time of kickoff.

The focus on the top-rated prospects is intense. The cultivation and solicitation of each advance gift needs to be carried out as if it were a mini-campaign by itself, according to a well-planned and carefully executed strategy. It may take two to three years or longer to raise the campaign nucleus fund, and patience is required.

Experts have differing views on how much of the overall campaign goal needs to be raised as part of the nucleus fund. In earlier decades, something between one-third and one-half was the standard, but in the 1990s and 2000s many campaigns had secured 40–50 percent or more of the goal by the time of public announcement and that has become an accepted industry standard. In a 2005 survey of private colleges and universities conducted by the Association of Governing Boards of Universities and Colleges (AGB), the median institution had raised just over 50 percent of its goal as part of the nucleus fund (Worth, 2005, p. 86).

Obviously, the more that has been raised in this period the greater the confidence that the announced goal will be achieved, but the subject is a little complicated. First, it depends on what is encompassed by the campaign's overall goal. For example, if the goal includes anticipated annual giving and program support over a total of seven years or more, it is unrealistic and unnecessary that 40–50 percent of those funds be already *committed* before the campaign is announced, although it is important that projections of such revenue over the period of the campaign be realistic. On the other hand, in light of the pattern of giving seen in recent campaigns, it is essential that a high percentage of the capital portion of the goal be committed early because just a handful of leadership gifts and advance gifts from the board may account for a substantial portion of the amount ultimately raised. In the 2005 AGB survey mentioned previously, on average, members of the board of trustees gave almost 20 percent of the campaign total and about 50 percent of the nucleus fund (Worth, 2005, p. 86). Again, that study was limited to private colleges and universities, some of which were relatively small.

CASE's (2009) campaign guidelines mention two different approaches that institutions take in defining the nucleus fund and offer guidance:

> One is to limit credit for gifts received in the advance-gifts phase to those given for featured objectives of the campaign—and not just all gifts received during the advance-gifts period. This approach serves to strengthen the focus of campaign efforts and eventual results. Another approach is to have a comprehensive advance-gifts phase, during which you count all gifts and pledges. If you adopt this approach, explain to institutional personnel and campaign volunteers that reported outcomes of the quiet phase are a combination of the true impact of the campaign effort as well as ongoing fundraising operations. (p. 85)

PHASE III: KICKOFF

The formal announcement of the campaign—the kickoff—is identified as a distinct phase of the campaign because it is the transition from the quiet phase to the public phase. It is the culmination of the work that has been accomplished in the preceding months or years and a critical juncture in the overall effort. The kickoff is often a historic event in the life of a college or university, somewhat akin to the celebration of a major anniversary. It is an excellent opportunity to tell the institution's story and focus attention on its traditions, strengths, and aspirations.

The kickoff of a campaign often includes one of the most ambitious events a college or university will plan and manage. For example, the kickoff of Carnegie Mellon's campaign ("Inspire Innovation: The Campaign for Carnegie Mellon University") in October 2008 attracted more than two thousand students, faculty, alumni, and friends and included exhibits focused on science and engineering projects, five bands, and a concluding fireworks and light show (Carnegie Mellon University, n.d.).

Some kickoffs go beyond a single event and become a major focus for the entire college or university community, on and off campus. For example, announcement of the University of California–Berkeley's campaign ("The Promise of Berkeley") in September 2008 was preceded by a week of events, including a music festival, a campus picnic, a poetry reading, and a concert, as well as seminars and panel discussions featuring Berkeley faculty (University of California–Berkeley, 2008).

Campaign announcements are often coordinated with alumni gatherings in various locations across the country and the world, sometimes participating through a webcast. The purpose of such high-visibility events is to direct attention not only on the campaign and its goals and priorities, but more broadly on the strengths and direction of the college or university. The kickoff focuses the passion of the institution's constituency around the messages and themes of the campaign.

The importance of managing expectations in the planning and quiet phases of the campaign has already been mentioned. Preannouncement communication about the campaign should strive to achieve balance between, on the one hand, building excitement about an ambitious goal and, on the other, generating rumors of even larger numbers. If that balance is achieved—and if the planning and quiet phases of the campaign have been well executed—it may be possible to announce a goal for the campaign that *exceeds* the by now widely known working goal.

Combined with the announcement of impressive leadership gifts, that approach can bring excitement and momentum to the campaign at the outset of its public phase. If expectations are allowed to run too high, however, announcement of a goal that is equivalent to the preliminary goal may seem anticlimactic. Announcing a goal less than the preliminary goal is likely to disappoint and may even create a sense of failure at the outset of the public phase. It is ironic that in the latter circumstance, the dollar goal might be achieved, but amidst a sense of disappointment, all because of an inadequate communication strategy. It is usually better to surprise on the upside all along the way.

The kickoff is the time for announcing the nucleus fund total and the leadership gifts comprising it. The ideal total must be large enough to give reassurance that the announced goal is achievable, but not so large as to imply that the campaign is essentially over. Donors of leadership gifts are publicly recognized at the kickoff, both at the event and in related communications. This is also an occasion to illustrate the impact of gifts to the campaign by telling the stories of students aided, faculty research advanced, and programs strengthened, helping to make the campaign's objectives both tangible and human. Recognition of nucleus fund donors and announcement of commitments from campus insiders, such as the faculty and trustees, helps to develop the credibility of the campaign as an institution-wide effort and establishes a rolling bandwagon that others may be motivated to board.

Some do argue that campaign kickoffs have become too elaborate and expensive and that, especially in economically uncertain times, they should be planned with somewhat greater restraint. That is a reasonable position. But, when well planned, smoothly executed, and effectively communicated, the kickoff of a campaign offers a rare and powerful opportunity to mobilize sentiment and gain visibility and understanding, with benefits to the college or university that go beyond the campaign itself. Well done, campaign kickoffs are simply magic!

PHASE IV: PUBLIC PHASE

Following the kickoff, the campaign is in its public phase, which in higher education campaigns typically lasts about five to six years. Campaign plans for some nonprofit organizations break down the public phase into a major gifts phase or special gifts phase, which immediately follows the kickoff for a period of months or years, and then a general gifts phase, when the campaign becomes a broad-based solicitation of the entire constituency. But comprehensive campaigns for colleges and universities usually do not have a general gifts phase; the ongoing annual fund is the vehicle through which most individuals who do not have the capacity for a major gift are asked to participate in the campaign. For the campaign's volunteer leaders, the president, and most members of the development staff, the public phase of the campaign is really a major gifts campaign. The focus of effort throughout the campaign remains on the cultivation and solicitation of prospects with the capacity to make a major commitment toward one of the campaign's capital objectives.

The beginning of the public phase, following the kickoff, is another time of risk in the campaign. With everyone who has been involved to that point—including volunteer leaders, the staff, and the president—somewhat exhausted from planning and preparation for the kickoff and gratified by the commitments made to the nucleus fund, there is the danger that the post-kickoff time will bring a lull. Indeed, some authors, for example, Bill McGoldrick and Paul Robell, define "The Plateau of Fatigue" as a distinctive phase of the campaign, coming right after the kickoff (McGoldrick and Robell, 2002). If such a plateau occurs, strong presidential leadership is needed to maintain the campaign's momentum and keep everyone focused on the years of intensive major gifts fundraising that still lie ahead.

Major gift prospects may include foundations, corporations, or individuals, but foundations and corporations tend to behave differently from individual donors. Their support may play an important part in achieving the overall goal of the comprehensive campaign, especially at research universities that receive significant research and programmatic grants, but most campaigns emphasize major gifts from individual donors. It is to that area that much of the president's time and effort is likely to be devoted during the public phase. When campaign priorities include endowment and facilities projects, the focus on individual major and planned gifts is especially necessary.

The definition of a major gift varies among institutions. A common definition is $100,000 or more, payable over a five-year pledge period, but for other institutions it may be more or less, depending on their fundraising history, the number of qualified prospects, and other variables. The term "principal gifts" has entered the fundraising vocabulary generally within the past fifteen years. For example, the phrase was absent from the 1993 book *Educational Fund Raising: Principles and Practice*, published by the American Council of Education (Worth, 1993), but it commanded a chapter in *New Strategies for Educational Fund Raising*, published by the American Council on Education in 2002 (Worth, 2002). In the latter volume, chapter author Frank Schubert defines principal gifts not only as large major gifts ("$5 million, $10 million, or even more"), but also as gifts that have a significant impact, that are "rare gifts in the life of an institution" (Schubert, 2002, p. 105). That is something like the concept of transformational gifts, which have such significant impact that they change the future of the college or university. They include many of the multimillion-dollar gifts and bequests that we read about in the *Chronicle of Higher Education*. But many institutions simply define principal gift prospects as those of the highest potential for the institution, requiring the priority attention of the president and, in larger development operations, a principal gifts officer or staff of professionals primarily dedicated to this portfolio of critical relationships.

Chapter 6 of this book, "Executing the Campaign," provides a more detailed discussion of the major gifts fundraising process that is at the heart of the campaign during the public phase and the president's role in it. The public phase is intense and often among the most draining for the president. The quiet phase is obviously of critical importance, and awaiting the decisions of key leadership prospects may be enough to keep the president awake. But in the public phase, prospects are engaged at higher volume. There is more travel and more events. These are days when presidents may fall asleep at yet another Marriott and dream about returning to the faculty!

PHASE V: CLOSING PHASE

The closing phase is really just the final months of the public phase of the campaign. It may be a time for revisiting prospects seen earlier in the campaign but who were not then ready to give. The approaching deadline may help to move some to a decision at this point. The closing phase may also be a time to focus on any of the campaign's objectives that have not yet been achieved, for example, specific building projects or perhaps endowment. Communication and solicitation may focus on specific constituencies with interest in those priorities or it may take on a regional focus. And, of course, planning for the victory celebration—another major event—needs to be under way as the campaign enters its final year.

The victory celebration is usually a major event, but not always of the same magnitude as the kickoff. Its purpose is not only to provide a punctuation mark to conclude the campaign. It is also an opportunity to highlight important campaign gifts and their impact on the college or university, recognize top donors and volunteer leaders, and just bask in the satisfaction of a major challenge having been successfully met. In addition to a final event, most campaigns publish a final summary report and other post-campaign communications, which are discussed more in chapter 9.

PHASE VI: POST-CAMPAIGN
EVALUATION, PLANNING, AND STEWARDSHIP

The post–victory celebration period is appropriately regarded as a phase of the campaign itself—and it is an important one. It is a time to examine lessons learned, analyze what worked and what did not. It is the time to continue active stewardship of campaign gifts and relationships with the donors who made them and to advance relationships with new donors and volunteers who may become leaders in a future campaign. This post-campaign period is so important, especially its stewardship component, that it is the focus of chapter 8 of this book.

Comprehensive campaigns today run over a period of years and encompass broad, complex goals and objectives. It is thus not uncommon that a campaign achieves its overall dollar goal but that some specific goals have not been fully met. For example, gifts for scholarship endowment may have exceeded the goal, but there may remain some unfunded professorships or capital projects for which additional support needs to be raised. Some of these priorities may be pursued through focused campaigns after the completion of the comprehensive effort. Some institutions also will rededicate their efforts to the annual fund and planned giving during the intercampaign period.

For many colleges and universities, the hiatus is not long. Planning for the next campaign often begins shortly after the victory celebration. Indeed, the interval between campaigns has shortened to the point that some authors say we are now in an era of virtually continuous campaigns, with most institutions either planning or executing a campaign all the time. Indeed, one answer to the critics of the campaign, who prefer a continuous major gifts program, is that ongoing major gifts fundraising is the reality at many colleges and universities today. In those cases, campaigns are really umbrellas of communication placed over certain time periods within that continuing effort. Proper management of post-campaign planning, stewardship, and communication is essential in this never-ending process. Assuring that critical post-campaign tasks are pursued is a responsibility of the president, whether or not he or she expects to be leading the institution's next comprehensive campaign.

REFERENCES

Carnegie Mellon University. (N.d.). "Celebrate Our Future." www.cmu.edu/campaign/involved/events.html (accessed February 24, 2009).

Chait, Richard P., William P. Ryan, and Barbara E. Taylor. (2005). *Governance as Leadership: Reframing the Work of Nonprofit Boards*. Washington, DC: BoardSource.

Council for Advancement and Support of Education (CASE). (2009). *CASE Reporting Standards and Management Guidelines*. 4th edition. Washington, DC: Author.

McGoldrick, William P., and Paul A. Robell. (2002). "Campaigning in the New Century." In Michael J. Worth (Ed.), *New Strategies for Educational Fund Raising*. Westport, CT: American Council on Education and Praeger, pp. 135–152.

Schubert, Frank D. (2002). "Principal Gifts." In Michael J. Worth (Ed.), *New Strategies for Educational Fund Raising*. Westport, CT: American Council on Education and Praeger, pp. 105–111.

Strout, Erin. (2007). "What's the Big Idea?" *Chronicle of Higher Education*, 53 (22), February 2, 2007, p. A21.

Thomsen, Tom. (2009). "Enhancing Capital Campaigns: The Advantages of Comprehensive Strategic Planning" [electronic document]. Marts & Lundy Special Report. www.martsandlundy.com/special_reports.php (accessed June 15, 2009).

University of California–Berkeley. (2008). "Events Mark Countdown to Campaign Kickoff." *Berkeleyan*, September 12. berkeley.edu/news/berkeleyan/2008/09/12_kickoff.shtml (accessed February 24, 2009).

Worth, Michael J. (Ed.). (1993). *Educational Fund Raising: Principles and Practice*. Phoenix: American Council on Education and the Oryx Press.

———. (Ed.). (2002). *New Strategies for Educational Fund Raising*. Westport, CT: American Council on Education and Praeger.

———. (2005). *Securing the Future: A Fund-Raising Guide for Boards of Independent Colleges and Universities*. Washington, DC: Association of Governing Boards of Universities and Colleges.

3

The Campaign Team

Some people seem to hold a great person theory of fundraising. That is, their comments suggest that a charismatic and tireless president—maybe something like the early college fund raisers discussed in chapter 1—should be enough to inspire gifts. But most successful campaigns reflect a team approach, and responsibility for success as well as any disappointment is shared among volunteer and campus leaders.

The president plays a central role as the institution's chief visionary and spokesperson; indeed, the president often becomes the personification of the institution in the minds of alumni and other donors. He or she will be a primary solicitor of gifts to the campaign and the president's ability to inspire and gain confidence is important. The president's judgment and consistency are essential to keep the campaign on track with its plan, to bring energy to the process if it hits a plateau, and to manage the potential conflicts that can arise in an intensive effort with high stakes and many high-achieving people involved.

But an effective campaign team also includes a committed board, other campaign volunteers, and experienced advancement staff. At universities, other campus executives, especially deans and directors, also play impor-tant roles, especially with regard to campaign priorities related to their particular college, school, or program. This chapter discusses models for organizing campaign leadership and the campaign roles of volunteers, the president, and the chief development or advancement officer.

VOLUNTEER AUTHENTICATORS

The active participation of volunteer leaders brings many benefits. Their engagement may deepen their commitment to the institution, calling forth their own generous support. Their relationships and access within the community or within their own professional and business circles may help to open doors and gain a hearing on the institution's case. The example of their leadership helps to set the standard for others. And they may be able to advocate the institution's cause with greater authenticity than campus leaders themselves.

When I was a university vice president for development and alumni relations, I witnessed the impact of a volunteer leader in one campaign solicitation that provided an important lesson and a lasting memory. I accompanied the campaign chair, Charlie, on a visit to a man named Bill, who was a prospect for a major gift to the campaign. (Both names are changed.) Charlie was a real estate developer and one of the most highly regarded leaders in his community. His vision and real estate projects were widely hailed as having transformed and revitalized the downtown of his city. He had been chair of the local board of trade and many charitable and business organizations. Bill was successful, too, but younger and not yet as accomplished.

When Charlie and I arrived to visit Bill at his office, the personal dynamics were obvious from the start. Bill greeted us at the elevator rather than have us wait in his lobby. He was obviously excited about having Charlie come to visit him and immediately began the conversation by telling Charlie about some of the real estate projects he was planning, obviously eager to impress and relate to Charlie as a peer. Bill was polite toward me, but clearly more intent on engaging Charlie.

Eventually, Charlie turned the discussion to the campaign and asked me to provide a summary of its goals and priorities, which I did. Without responding, Bill turned right back to Charlie and continued the discussion of the local real estate market. Indeed, Bill preempted Charlie's ability to ask for the gift, which had been our plan. I wondered if I had said something wrong. But, eventually, Bill came around to the subject of the visit, turning to me and saying, "I am not ignoring you, and your summary of the campaign was a good one. . . . You do your job well," he added, to my relief. Turning again to Charlie, he went on, "I had decided to make a gift before you came, but I need to tell you, Charlie, how impressed I am that you have taken the time to come out here to visit me. This campaign must be important to you and I admire what you are doing for the university. Let me go back tonight and talk to my wife and see if we can increase what we had planned to do. I know we can't give as much as you have, but we'll see if we can find a way to come closer." The meeting ended with Bill walking Charlie to the elevator, again engaged in real estate talk, while I basically trailed along.

The next day, Bill called Charlie and made a commitment larger than we had expected, and larger than he previously had planned to make. He said again how impressed he was by Charlie's involvement. The obvious critical difference had been Charlie's influence on Bill. As Bill had pointed out, I had "done [my] job," and apparently "well." I was certainly as able as anyone else to summarize the case and explain the goals and priorities of the campaign. *But information is not enough.* It was the demonstration of Charlie's selfless and real commitment to the campaign that inspired Bill and the social relationship between them that motivated him to stretch. Who is speaking is sometimes just as important as what they say. It was Charlie's leadership that made the university's appeal to Bill both authentic and compelling.

INVOLVING VOLUNTEER LEADERSHIP

The institution's own planning may begin with an internal committee, but as emphasized in chapter 2, engaging trustees and other volunteers at an appropriate point helps establish their ownership of the outcome. Members of the governing board do, of course, have responsibility for the programs and directions of the college or university, so their involvement in planning is appropriate so long as it does not encroach on the academic prerogatives of the faculty. The board of an affiliated foundation has fiduciary responsibility for the foundation's assets, but not for the institution itself, so the involvement of its members in institutional planning requires care and judgment. In most universities there also are a variety of advisory boards or councils associated with its colleges, schools, and research units, which may play an important role in planning. Again, their involvement requires due attention to what is appropriate.

In a 2007 study of advisory councils at public and private colleges and universities, conducted by the Association of Governing Boards of Universities and Colleges (AGB), some deans suggested that the input of their advisory councils was important in strategic planning as part of the "environmental scan." That is, they said that members of their advisory councils were able to bring important insights from the industries and professions in which they worked, helping to inform the school's plans and goals. But some deans also emphasized that care must be taken to assure that advisory councils do not become too deeply involved in curriculum or other academic matters that belong to the faculty or in matters of institutional governance or finance that are the responsibility of the governing board (Worth, 2008).

Once the focus has begun to shift from institutional planning to the campaign planning, the circle of involvement expands with the creation of a campaign planning committee. Membership of this committee generally includes the president, the chief academic officer, the chief development officer, the chief financial officer, and perhaps other internal members, such as one or two deans of major schools. It also engages key trustees, usually including the chair of the board and the chair of the development or advancement committee, and perhaps a few others. It may also come to include other volunteer leaders who are viewed as likely leaders of the campaign itself. The committee must be small enough to be an effective working group, but also inclusive enough to provide the opportunity of involving key volunteers at the earliest stage of the campaign.

The responsibility of the campaign planning committee, with leadership from its chair, the president, and the chief development officer, is to guide the process of preparing for the campaign, which is discussed further in chapters 4 and 5. That preparartion includes developing the preliminary goal and objectives, establishing campaign policies, determining the budget for the campaign, deciding on the structure of volunteer leadership, and endorsing the preliminary case statement and campaign plan. The committee must decide what type of market test to undertake, if any, advise that study, and reach decisions based upon its results.

A key responsibility of the campaign planning committee is to identify and enlist the top volunteer leadership of the campaign, which may or may not come from within its own membership. The campaign planning committee has a time-limited role; it disbands when the campaign leadership is appointed. But there is usually some rollover of key individuals from the planning committee to leadership positions in the campaign itself.

At some colleges and universities, the board's standing committee on development or advancement may also play the role of the campaign planning committee and, ultimately, the campaign leadership committee as well. But AGB's 2004 study of independent colleges and universities found that 72 percent of institutions establish a separate committee to lead the campaign. The principal reasons cited for doing so include the desire to involve campaign leaders from outside the board itself and to keep the board's development committee focused on general advancement policy and strategy (Worth, 2005, p. 97).

The board's committee on development or advancement is a standing committee of the board, with ongoing responsibilities beyond the campaign. They include assuring that fundraising goals and priorities are aligned with mission and academic plans, monitoring the institution's overall fundraising program, and establishing policies with regard to such matters as the acceptance of gifts. Members of the standing development committee may be donors and may be involved as individual trustees in the cultivation and solicitation of prospects. But direct involvement in fundraising is not the responsibility of the committee *as a committee*. The development committee has an ongoing oversight and policy role, an ongoing *institutional* responsibility that differs from the more focused assignment of a campaign leadership committee. In addition, most board committees are really committees on advancement that are concerned with the institution's communications, marketing, and alumni relations programs, as well as fundraising and the campaign. That may require membership on the advancement committee of individuals who are not able to participate significantly in fundraising, for example, perhaps the president of the alumni association or a trustee with experience in the communications profession.

But having a campaign leadership committee separate from the board's standing committee on development or advancement requires clarity about responsibilities and roles. To illustrate, AGB's 2004 study of independent colleges and universities found that campaign committees were involved in developing fundraising and gift-acceptance policies in 50 percent of responding institutions and that 52 percent of campaign committees were involved in "ensuring that the institution's fundraising program is aligned with its mission and planning priorities" (Worth, 2005, p. 99). But matters of institutional policies, mission, and priorities are governing board matters. To be formal about things, campaign decisions that rise to a matter of institutional policy should run from the campaign leadership committee to the development or advancement committee and from that committee to the full board for action. Of course, how this works in practice will depend to some extent on the individuals involved in these various roles and the relationships among them. There is often an overlap of membership among these groups. Many campaign chairs are also members of the board and the chair of the development committee usually sits on the campaign committee. That facilitates communication and clarity, although it still may be necessary for individuals to remember which hat they are wearing as certain questions are discussed and resolved. The situation may be especially sensitive at public colleges and universities where the board of an affiliated foundation is also the principal leadership of the campaign.

ORGANIZING CAMPAIGN LEADERSHIP

Historically, it was typical to have a single campaign chair, who usually was an influential member of the board and also a top donor to the campaign. He or she, together with the president and the board chair, enlisted other leaders of the campaign, participated in the solicitation of advance gifts, and presided over the campaign for its duration. The campaign chair was often someone like Charlie (in my previous campaign anecdote), a leader who is universally recognized and admired throughout the institution's community. Such individuals still exist and are the leaders of many campaigns. But alternative patterns of campaign leadership also have emerged in recent decades.

Especially in large university campaigns that extend over several years, with ambitious and comprehensive goals that encompass multiple academic units, it may be more challenging than in the past to enlist a single chair who will accept such a large and enduring responsibility. Many may prefer to share the load with others as co-chairs of the campaign. In addition to spreading the burden, enlisting co-chairs assures that campaign leadership is representative of the institution's various constituencies and the regions and professions in which its prospective donors live and work.

For example, Cornell's campaign ("Far Above: The Campaign for Cornell") was launched in 2006 with three co-chairs, representing different generations of alumni and including one co-chair focused on the Weill Cornell Medical College (Ashley, Zubrow, and Appel, 2009). The University of Maryland–College Park kicked off its $1 billion campaign ("Great Expectations: The Campaign for Maryland") in 2006 with five co-chairs reflecting a diversity of backgrounds and professions (University of Maryland, 2008). And Berkeley's campaign, announced in 2008 ("The Promise of Berkeley") was led by seven co-chairs, including three couples (University of California–Berkeley, 2008). The co-chair approach is an effective way to highlight the comprehensive nature of a college or university and bring together diverse academic units, alumni generations, and far-flung alumni in a unified effort under common themes.

Some campaigns also identify honorary chairs. This is a good practice if the honorary chairs are of such stature that people would notice their absence, but they cannot be expected to take an active role in the campaign for reasons that are obvious, perhaps their age or position. On the other hand, if the reasons why honorary leaders must be honorary are not so obvious, listing them may actually send a negative message, possibly suggesting that their commitment to the cause is tepid or that the active leaders of the campaign are the second string.

One question that often surfaces when the discussion turns to enlisting the campaign chair or co-chairs is the level of financial commitment that should be expected from the individual or individuals accepting that role. Traditional thinking was that the ideal campaign chair would also make the top gift, thus setting an example and empowering him or her to solicit gifts from others at all levels. The underlying principle was that a volunteer solicitor could ask only for a gift equal to or less than his or her own commitment and thus the campaign chair needed to be at the top. But those standards have changed for many reasons. The largest campaign gifts may come from donors who, for various reasons, are unable to play an active leadership role in the campaign. Although major gifts remain the largest element of campaigns, campaign leadership also needs to be representative of the institution's broader constituency in order to meet its goals for broad-based support and communication. The campaign chair or co-chairs are generally expected to make gifts that are widely recognized as sacrificial for them, that is, proportional to their capacity. But they need not be the top gifts in the campaign so long as the other conditions of leadership are met.

Campaign Steering Committee

Overall direction of the campaign is provided by a senior leadership committee, which may be identified by various terms. In this book, it is called the campaign steering committee, but other terms are used.

In a campaign for a small college, the steering committee may be the extent of the campaign organization. It may encompass several people, including perhaps the board chair, the chair of the development or advancement committee, the campaign chair or co-chairs, the campaign vice chair or co–vice chairs, possibly a few other members of the board, the president, and the chief development officer. The steering committee is responsible for campaign strategy and policy, but may also play a hands-on role in the cultivation and solicitation of top donors, especially for advance gifts during the quiet phase.

In larger campaigns, the steering committee may include all of the above plus the chairs of various additional committees focused on particular components of the campaign. In this expanded format, the steering committee may discuss a relatively small number of top prospects but be primarily focused on campaign strategy, policy, and coordination. Much of the on-the-ground fundraising may involve other committees leading components of the overall campaign.

A larger steering committee may be needed to assure consistency, coordination, and communication across the breadth of a comprehensive, and possibly decentralized, campaign. In that situation there may also be a need for a smaller group of key leaders drawn from the steering committee—a campaign executive committee—that can meet more frequently and respond quickly when key decisions must be made. The executive committee may include just the board chair, campaign chair or co-chairs, development committee chair, the president, the chief development officer, and perhaps one or two others.

Campaign Committee Organization

Again, in smaller institutions, the campaign steering committee may fulfill most or all of the need for volunteer leadership. But in larger campaigns, especially at universities with multiple colleges and schools and constituents across the nation or the world, there will be a need for a more extensive campaign organization. Campaign committees are organized according to four basic models.

1. *By gift level or phase.* Sometimes committees are organized according to the level of giving and/or phase of the campaign. For example, there may be an advance gifts committee that is active in the quiet phase, a major gifts committee that focuses on soliciting major gifts during the public phase, and an annual fund committee, which, as its name suggests, works to achieve goals for annual giving during the campaign period.
2. *By source of support.* In other campaigns, committees are organized according to sources of anticipated support. There may be committees focused on corporate support, foundation support, individual giving, planned giving, and specific constituencies, such as parents, alumni, and faculty and staff.
3. *By academic unit, project, or priority.* In comprehensive campaigns at universities, there are often committees focused on particular academic or administrative units and/or on specific projects or program areas, for example, athletics or student life.
4. *By geography.* A fourth way to organize campaign committees is by geography, for example, with committees in cities where the institution has large concentrations of alumni. Regional committees usually exist in addition to one of the other three basic models.

The model or models adopted depend on the institution's structure, the size and distribution of its constituencies, and political realities. Most campaign organizations show a blend or adaptation of the approaches described here, and there are many variations in vocabulary and job descriptions. Some are relatively simple structures, but others are more elaborate. For example, the leadership of Southern Methodist University's (SMU) campaign "The Second Century Campaign" includes a fifteen-member campaign leadership council, with responsibility for soliciting leadership gifts in the quiet phase and then providing general oversight of the public phase, more or less a combination of an advance gifts committee and campaign steering committee as described previously. Members of that council are identified as co-chairs of the campaign. SMU's campaign steering committee encompasses the co-chairs for each of SMU's major academic units as well as other campaign priorities, including athletics and student life. This steering committee also includes co-chairs focused on several national and international regions of importance to SMU (Southern Methodist University, 2009).

The volunteer organization should be what is needed and not more. It is possible to make a mistake by building a structure that is too large and too complex, then filling boxes on the chart with people who require support but who may bring little added impact to the campaign effort. That can lead to advancement staff and even the president becoming mired in communication and relationships with volunteers, leaving too little time or energy for fundraising. It is important to recognize that while volunteers are not paid, they also are not free. A campaign organization may involve dozens or hundreds of volunteers and requires adequate campaign staff to support it. Essential as they are to a successful campaign, volunteers will not be effective if they are left without clear direction, support, and communication.

The organization of volunteer leadership for the campaign needs to be a good fit with the history, culture, and constituency of the college or university. For a university with strong professional schools—especially law, medicine, and business—it usually makes sense to have committees focused on the goals and constituencies of those particular units as part of the overall campaign organization. But it may not be useful to have a committee for every academic unit, especially if some are small, young, or lacking in major gift prospects. That may result in a large campaign steering committee with members who face very different challenges in their fundraising leadership, perhaps making it difficult to have mutually rewarding discussions or achieve consensus. Of course, this concern must be weighed against the risk of sending a negative message to units that are not represented or engendering criticism from their constituents. Again, a larger steering committee may require an executive committee that is more selective and that can make some decisions without too much consultation and discussion.

Regional committees may be important for a university that has active alumni in cities across the country. Colleges that find most of their alumni within their own communities or the radius of a one-day trip, they may find that such committees require added time and expense with little marginal return. Organizing by graduation class may make sense for an undergraduate college, if its alumni have a strong sense of class identity, but may add infrastructure without benefit at a university where most alumni received graduate degrees or attended part time.

It is not useful to draw a complex organizational chart if, in reality, there are only a small number of effective volunteers available for the total campaign.

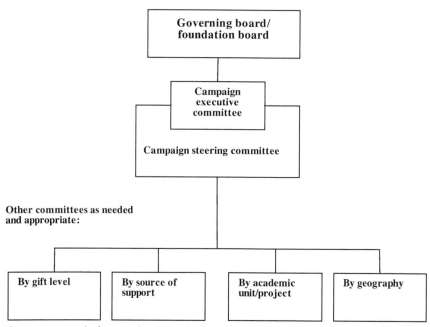

Figure 3.1. Typical Campaign Organization

That can only lead to diluting the quality of campaign leadership. The benefits of broader involvement need to be measured against the costs in time and resources.

It can be a problem if a board member, consultant, or someone else tries to impose a model that he or she has seen work successfully in a campaign at another institution that has different characteristics. The president needs to understand the potential and the pitfalls of any organizational model suggested for the campaign and evaluate its effectiveness in the specific setting for which it is proposed.

Figure 3.1 depicts a campaign organization along the lines discussed here, but again, it is important to recognize that there are many variations in structure and terminology in use.

UNDERSTANDING CAMPAIGN ROLES:
AN UNUSUAL FOOTBALL TEAM

Organizational charts depict the formal relationships among positions but do not explain the roles of the individuals who occupy the boxes. Indeed, titles may incorrectly imply authority or passivity; what does it really mean to "chair" or "steer" or "lead?"

The fundraising partnership of volunteers (especially the board), the president, and the chief advancement officer has been the focus of a number of authors. Writing in the 1980s, William Kinnison and Michael Ferin outline a job description for each of the three parties. They identify the board's responsibilities as ensuring that fundraising efforts align with the institution's mission and priorities; monitoring the fundraising budget and staff; coordinating trustee activity with the president and chief development officer; and becoming personally involved in the fundraising process. They write that the president's responsibilities include providing leadership in defining and articulating the mission; forging links between development professionals and the board; providing support for the board's involvement in fundraising; and becoming personally involved in the fundraising process. Finally, Kinnison and Ferin describe the chief development officer's responsibilities as facilitating the president's and trustees' fundraising activities through information, training, and preparation; providing an effective teamwork environment; translating mission, priorities, and needs into a case statement and campaign plan; and becoming personally involved in the fundraising process (Kinnison and Ferin, 1989).

More recent authors mention many of the same responsibilities, with some refinements. For example, writing in 2002, Sara Patton describes the board's involvement in identifying, cultivating, and soliciting gifts as well as setting an example through their own support. Like Kinnison and Ferin, she discusses the president's responsibility to articulate the mission and a vision of the future and to facilitate relationships between the board and staff. Reflecting the changes than occurred in fundraising from the 1980s to the 2000s, which included an increased role for development officers in soliciting major gifts, Patton also adds the need for chief development officers to balance their responsibilities for supporting the president and board with their own direct engagement of prospects and donors (Patton, 2002).

But such terms as "ensuring," "facilitating," and "articulating" are still not quite specific. In *Securing the Future*, published by the AGB, I tried to bring some operational understanding to the fundraising partnership by describing the key players in the campaign as an unusual kind of football team (Worth, 2005). The book was based on a study conducted by the AGB of the governing board's role in fundraising at independent colleges and universities. The situation is, of course, somewhat more complicated at public institutions, where, in addition to the governing board, there is often a board with responsibility for an affiliated foundation that may be the most active with regard to the campaign. In the following discussion, references to "the board" mean whichever board is primarily responsible for the campaign.

The vocabulary of fundraising is drawn from sports and the military. A campaign (the term itself a military concept) begins like a football game, with a kickoff. Like a war, it ends with a victory celebration. To be sure, campaigns can be intense. But a football game seems to provide a more appropriate metaphor than war. Football also seems to offer a better metaphor than some other sports.

In baseball, much of the time, attention is focused on the individual performance of just two people—the pitcher and the catcher. Indeed, statistics of the game are largely based on the performance of individual players. That is sometimes the situation in fundraising, but thinking that way also may lead to the great person theory mentioned previously, that is, the generally unrealistic expectation that the president, dean, or chief development officer should be hitting home runs.

Basketball involves teamwork, but the game really only progresses when somebody scores a basket. The crowd usually holds its reaction as the ball moves around the court and erupts in cheers only when it goes through the net.

In football, there are more opportunities for fans to cheer intermediate successes between scores, as the team makes progress on individual downs, in yardage gained, and in passes completed. The end result of every game depends, of course, on scoring points, but in football and in fundraising, that result may come only after the execution of several plays, each of which is an achievement in itself. There is nothing in football, or in fundraising, that is quite comparable to a home run or a three-point shot.

Members of the board are analogous to the owners of a professional football team. That is, they have responsibility for the overall success of the franchise. They are expected to ensure that the enterprise is financially viable and achieves the goals that the owners have established. Owners invest in the team. They hire coaches, trainers, and players and evaluate their performance. But unlike game day in the NFL, in a campaign the owners are expected to come down out of their sky boxes and participate on the field. That is, they are expected to go beyond their usual policy-making role and become active participants in fundraising.

The president holds four jobs on this unusual team. He or she may be a member of the governing or foundation board and is thus an owner. The president is also like the manager—he or she hires at least some of the players. The president is also like the coach, sometimes guiding and pushing members of the team, including board members, to their own maximum performance. And, finally, the president is sometimes the star runner; he or she often carries the fundraising football, scores a touchdown, inspires the fans, and is among the most visible players on the field. It is a complex role that requires exceptional executive and athletic ability.

The chief development officer, or the director of the campaign, is like a quarterback. He or she calls plays, sometimes runs the ball, and at other times hands it off or passes it to other players. The job is complicated, too, because the players often include the owners and the coach.

In addition to being wise owners, board members need to be versatile athletes. Sometimes they run the ball themselves. Sometimes they accept handoffs or receive passes from the quarterback. Sometimes they are blockers, whose job it is to create an opening for the president or the chief development officer to run through. But the game cannot be played successfully without them. A coach and a quarterback alone on the field would be unlikely to make it to the playoffs.

Some presidents may sometimes try to run the ball alone. So may some development officers. The outcome is usually what one would expect. They are cheered when they make a touchdown, but booed when they fail to score. There is a higher probability of injury in playing the game solo than in making the game a team effort in which responsibility for winning is shared.

This discussion so far has focused on the board—again, whichever board is most relevant to the campaign at a given institution. But a campaign engages volunteer leaders beyond the board itself. Depending on the size and scope of the institution and the campaign, the volunteer organization may involve a large number of people. But it is important that members of the board be in prominent positions of leadership in the campaign and that the volunteer leadership organization be seen as essentially an extension of the board. Members of the governing board are the owners of the effort, and if they are not seen as deeply committed to its success, it is difficult to envision others bringing much energy to the game.

To complete this football analogy, I mention an occasion a few years ago when I described it in a presentation to an assembly of presidents from the sixty-four campuses of the State University of New York at the system headquarters in Albany. When I concluded, the chancellor of the system asked me, "What is the system's role in this game?" I quickly responded, "You are the NFL, you establish the rules under which the teams can play." He smiled, but followed up, "So, what is the role of fundraising consultants?" My wit failed me and I hesitated, so one of the presidents offered a response: "I think they are like the sports commentators," he said. "They are always talking but they have no impact on the game." He was smiling, so I was sure he meant it as a joke.

BUILDING AND MAINTAINING TEAM RELATIONSHIPS

Building and maintaining strong working relationships among the members of a team is, of course, essential to success in any endeavor. The campaign team may present some unusual complexity.

To use the phrase that Richard Chait and his coauthors apply to college and university governing boards, the campaign organization brings together "part-time amateurs and full-time professionals" (Chait, Holland, and Taylor, 1996, p. 3). Volunteer leaders of the campaign are not development professionals. They may have some experience as volunteers in other campaigns at other, possibly very different, organizations or institutions. But they may not have extensive knowledge about campaign management or perhaps a full appreciation of the differences between philanthropic fundraising and commercial sales. Their involvement in setting campaign strategy may at times be a source of frustration to fundraising professionals, who have specialized skills and knowledge, to which some volunteer leaders may not always defer. The professionals also may be frustrated by the need to work with volunteers' crowded calendars and other obligations, which sometimes delay the scheduling of campaign meetings or solicitations.

Campaign staff members are focused on the campaign all the time and may sometimes interpret volunteers' distraction by other demands as a lack of commitment to the effort and be tempted to move ahead without them. At the same time, volunteer leaders may sometimes feel that the professional staff members ask too much of them or do not adequately prepare to make the best use of their precious time. Volunteers who are successful people in their own fields may not appreciate a tone or style that suggests their subordination to staff direction or action by the staff that ignores their advice with regard to prospects they know.

Melding together an effective team of people with different backgrounds, experiences, and incentives is often a challenge. But college and university presidents are called upon to do this all the time. Presidents often need to motivate, negotiate, and inspire within their institutions, in order to forestall controversies and maintain progress toward common goals. They are often called upon to bridge the academic and business worlds, educating each with regard to the values of the other. Both volunteer leaders and development staff are essential members of the campaign team. Building and maintaining relationships among the team and keeping it moving forward toward the goal line is an essential part of leadership, for football coaches and for presidents.

THE PRESIDENT AND THE CHIEF DEVELOPMENT OFFICER

There is perhaps no relationship more critical to the success of a fundraising program than the partnership between the president and his or her chief development or advancement officer. Most work together effectively and well. But, there are cases in which that partnership is not working as smoothly as it should. The result may be frequent turnover in the development office and a loss of continuity in fundraising efforts and relationships with donors. That can be highly detrimental if it occurs during a campaign. Many partnerships can be strengthened by directly addressing two common issues.

Clarification of Roles

Development officers play various roles, as discussed in the preceding football analogy. Some are strong outside people, that is, effective in cultivating and soliciting donors directly. Some are excellent strategists but not as good at executing plays. Others may work better behind the scenes, supporting fundraising conducted by volunteers and the president. Some are good at managing the development office; others have excellent people skills but are not as strong on administrative details. Most are required to play each of these roles at some point and some may be good at all of them. But most are relatively stronger in some than in others.

Which roles are most important in a given situation may depend, in part, on the relative strengths and weaknesses of the president and the depth of volunteer involvement in fundraising, among other factors. But how often are these roles discussed explicitly in preemployment interviews between presidents and development candidates? How many share a common understanding of what skills the chief development officer position actually requires at a specific institution at a particular time? Before accepting a development position, candidates should ask the questions "How do you see the role of the chief development officer?" "What skills do you think a person needs to succeed in this position?" and "What do you think are your own strengths and weaknesses and how can a chief development officer best support you?" Eager for the job, candidates may fail to ask these questions. Eager to fill the position, presidents may fail to think about the answers.

Working Relationship

The president and the chief development officer inevitably must spend a fair amount of time together. And the chief development needs to be able to speak for the president. He or she thus needs some intuitive understanding of how the president thinks. The president and chief development officer need to talk about their work together and do so regularly. A standing meeting, at least once a week, offers opportunities for such conversations and should occur even if there is no specific agenda. It is often in the unstructured conversations, in which they brainstorm together or think out loud with each other, that the president and development officer come to understand each other's preferences, styles, thought processes, and other qualities that are central to a solid working relationship. Some may find it easy to cancel such meetings when there is no immediate business to discuss. But unstructured meetings are not a waste of time. Spending regular time together is important to assuring that the team continues to function smoothly.

The relationship between the president and the chief development or advancement officer is crucial. They are among the most important players on the team. The intensity and stresses that inevitably accompany a campaign require that this relationship receive deliberate time and thoughtful attention.

REFERENCES

Ashley, Stephen, Jan Rock Zubrow, and Robert J. Appel. (2009). "Message from the Chairs 2009." Cornell University. www.campaign.cornell.edu/chairs_message.cfm (accessed March 5, 2009).

Chait, Richard P., Thomas P. Holland, and Barbara E. Taylor. (1996). *Improving the Performance of Governing Boards.* Phoenix: American Council on Education and the Oryx Press.

Kinnison, William A., and Michael J. Ferin. (1989). "The Three-Party Relationship." In *Fund-Raising Leadership: A Guide for College and University Boards.* Washington, DC: Association of Governing Boards of Universities and Colleges, pp. 57–61.

Patton, Sara L. (2002). "The Role of Key Individuals." In Michael J. Worth (Ed.), *New Strategies for Educational Fund Raising.* Phoenix: American Council on Education and Praeger, pp. 65–72.

Southern Methodist University. (2009). "Campaign Leadership Council." www.smu.edu/SecondCentury/Volunteers/CampaignLeadershipCouncil.aspx (accessed March 5, 2009).

University of California–Berkeley. (2008). "Campaign Leadership." promise.berkeley.edu/fall_2008/campaign_leadership/ (accessed March 7, 2009).

University of Maryland. (2008). "Campaign Leadership." www.greatexpectations.umd.edu/leadership.html (accessed March 5, 2009).

Worth, Michael J. (2005). *Securing the Future: A Fund-Raising Guide for Boards of Independent Colleges and Universities.* Washington, DC: Association of Governing Boards of Universities and Colleges.

———. (2008). *Sounding Boards: Advisory Councils in Higher Education.* Washington, DC: Association of Governing Boards of Universities and Colleges.

4

Campaign Goals, Priorities, and Objectives

Together, chapters 4 and 5 describe the key decisions that need to be addressed during Phase I, the planning phase, in order to be ready to formally launch the campaign. This chapter discusses the tasks of defining and articulating the case for support; evaluating the pool of donor prospects; and establishing goals, priorities, and objectives for the campaign. Chapter 5 considers the determination of budget and staff resources required for the campaign and important campaign policies that need to be established. Two chapters are devoted to the planning phase because it is especially important. As in building a house, it is critical to devote sufficient time and attention to design and to establishing a sound foundation. If those tasks are not done well, it may not be possible to go back and correct the errors at a later stage.

The planning phase takes the institution to the beginning of advance gift solicitation in the quiet phase. That is not to imply, however, that discussions with prospects do not begin until all of the planning has been completed; indeed, some prospects are likely included in the campaign planning process, and there is an ongoing dialogue between the college or university and its volunteer leaders and donor prospects. Leaders' evolving relationships with the institution will influence the campaign plan, and their involvement in preparing for the campaign will influence those relationships. Campaigns do not proceed in a linear or mechanistic way. They are organic; they grow, gain energy, and evolve as the process unfolds.

CAMPAIGN READINESS

Campaign planning is the process of *getting ready* to launch the campaign. A number of authors have suggested criteria for assessing readiness, in other words, prerequisites for campaign success. Some checklists produce a numerical readiness score (See, for example, Dove, 2000, p. 33; Pierpont, 2003, p. 137). But many situations are complex, and a single total score may obscure the finer points. A preliminary readiness assessment may be most useful as a vehicle for identifying relative strengths and weaknesses and the work that needs to be done to prepare for a campaign—that is, as a guide to planning—rather than as a standard by which to make a go/no-go decision.

The following criteria are similar to those articulated by various other authors and describe conditions that define ideal circumstances under which a college or university embarks upon a campaign.

- The institution has a clear vision of its mission, its place in higher education, and unique qualities that set it apart from others in terms of its impact on society, that is, it has a strong case for support.
- The institution has a plan for its future growth and improvement that is based on academic priorities.
- Specific fundraising goals and objectives have been identified, rooted in the institution's strategic priorities, as articulated in the plan.
- Major objectives of the proposed campaign are well understood internally and enjoy a broad consensus among trustees, campus leaders, faculty, staff, and other stakeholders at various levels.
- Members of the governing (and/or the foundation) board are committed to the institution's plan and the goals of the campaign and are prepared to support the campaign with time, energy, and personal resources, commensurate with their ability.
- The president is well regarded, is willing to commit a sufficient amount of time to the campaign, and is able to articulate the importance of the campaign's priorities.
- Other administrative leaders of the institution, for example, deans and program directors, are supportive of the campaign and willing to play appropriate roles, including participation in the cultivation and solicitation of prospects with interest in their units or activities.
- The institution has identified potential volunteer leaders of the campaign who are committed to its purposes, who are well known and respected in its constituency, who are prepared to commit sufficient time to leading the campaign, and who preferably are experienced in fundraising.

- There are prospects who have the capacity to make leadership gifts totaling a significant portion of the anticipated campaign goal (and who have been cultivated to a point of readiness to make such commitments).
- There are a sufficient number of prospects who have links to the institution, who have a known or demonstrated commitment to its purposes, and who have the financial capacity to provide the gifts required to attain the balance of the proposed goal.
- The institution has adequate knowledge (including records, prospect research, and other information) regarding the interests, philanthropic priorities, and life and financial circumstances of its prospects, in order to formulate solicitation strategies that will be timely and appropriate.
- The advancement or development office is led by a fundraising professional who serves as a senior officer of the organization, is well regarded by the governing board and/or foundation board, has access to the president and board members, and preferably has significant campaign experience.
- The development staff is sufficient in size, is properly configured, and possesses the experience and skills to execute a campaign.
- Fundraising information systems and services, including prospect research, are adequate to support a campaign.
- The development office has established relationships with such specialists, either internal or external, as may be needed during the campaign, for example, fundraising counsel, planned giving counsel, and professionals in communications, publications, and event management.
- Adequate budgetary resources have been committed to the campaign.
- There are no conditions affecting the institution that will have a negative impact on the campaign, for example, recent controversies, internal political divisions, or competing fundraising efforts among units within the campus or system.
- There are no conditions in the external environment that will have a negative impact on the campaign, for example, a poor economy or competing campaigns by other organizations in the same community.

Some of these conditions can, of course, be created as a part of preparing for the campaign. The institution can engage in planning to identify its priorities, hire development staff, engage external advisers, and commit resources to fundraising operations and systems.

Some conditions—a weak economy, the presence of competing campaigns, or some event in the life of the institution, for example, a recent turnover in the presidency or a key staff position—are mostly relevant for timing of the campaign.

But some circumstances are not controllable, at least not in the short term. They may affect the magnitude and/or the timing of the campaign. If the college or university has a limited pool of prospects, perhaps because of its history, location, or the types of programs it offers, that may cap what is a realistic goal. There may be additional prospects who have not yet been identified, some whose financial capacity has been underestimated, or others who have the ability to give but whose interest has yet to be fully developed. There may be potential in some of those circumstances. But if such prospects simply do not exist, then the goal of the campaign must either be appropriately modest or it represents wishful thinking.

The institution's prospect pool today is in part an image of its past, projected onto its current fundraising environment. For example, a college or university that thirty years ago primarily prepared students to be teachers and public servants may have alumni who are now in their fifties or older with distinguished career achievement. But many of them may not have accumulated significant wealth. The institution's programs may today look quite different from those of thirty years ago and include some that prepare students for more lucrative careers such as business and engineering. But graduates of those programs may still be relatively young and in the midst of family responsibilities that preclude a major gift. Someone looking at the institution's current academic profile—and perhaps comparing it to another institution that has similar programs today—might assume that there is a deeper pool of capable prospects among the alumni body than in fact there is, because of these historical realities.

Some institutions, especially independent colleges and universities, may have a long tradition of fundraising and philanthropy, possibly encompassing multiple generations of families. But some public institutions have established organized fundraising programs more recently and do not have a deep culture of philanthropy. Some may enroll students who are the first of their families to attend college, so they may not have traditions of giving to their educational institutions. That does not preclude a successful campaign, but it is a reality that needs to be considered in setting an achievable goal.

In 2008, the twenty institutions reporting the largest total of support were about half independent and half public, reflecting the substantial growth in private support of public institutions that has been a hallmark of the past forty years (Voluntary Support, 2008, p. 18). But it is instructive that, with the exception of the University of North Carolina at Chapel Hill, all of the public institutions on the list were in California or the Midwest. That reflects the historical strength of independent higher education in eastern states and the fact that many public institutions in those states began organized fundraising only within the past few decades.

And, finally, location plays a role. A college in a small town or rural environment may be able to attract support from its alumni but have few corporate prospects. A university in an urban area may find that its alumni have less emotional attachment to the campus than those of small colleges in more bucolic settings, but it may find support from foundations interested in its research and corporations that hire its graduates. It may receive support from local citizens who appreciate its impact on the local economy and culture. A community college may find that some of its alumni have a greater interest in four-year institutions that they later attended, but it may find support from local businesses and leaders who appreciate the college's importance to the local community. In sum, all of the contours of the institution's situation, both historically and currently, need to be considered in determining the goal, priorities, and timing of the campaign.

DEVELOPING A STRONG CASE

Successful fundraising begins with a case. A strong case for support reaches beyond the needs or ambitions of the college or university itself and is rooted in fundamental social and human problems, issues, or opportunities that the institution addresses. A good case is rooted in the essence of the institution—its mission, values, and vision of the future—and requires more than a list of "needs." A campaign that is perceived as the president's agenda, or that looks like a random collection of projects cobbled together by the development office, is unlikely to engender commitment. As discussed earlier in this book, broad participation in institutional and campaign planning is helpful to build understanding and a sense of ownership of the campaign among various constituencies, including the trustees and other major donor prospects. That may not mean formal strategic planning, which has its fans as well as critics, but it does mean more than a creative writing assignment for someone in the development or communications office.

It is important to distinguish the case for support—the rationale for giving—from two documents that are often produced: the case statement and the principal campaign publication (whether printed or electronic or both). The case statement is an internal document that includes comprehensive information about the institution, the campaign, and the objectives. It is sometimes called the "internal case statement" to distinguish it from publications intended for the outside audience. A case statement may be dry and full of facts. The principal campaign publication or brochure is more emotional in its tone and includes exciting visual images. The latter is sometimes called the "external case statement" to distinguish it from the former. Chapter 9 includes a further discussion of campaign communication materials.

The case for support is not the same as the case statement—it is more abstract—it does not include specific funding objectives or gift opportunities—and it should be capable of expression in no more than a few paragraphs.

A strong case starts outside the institution, with fundamental human problems, issues, and aspirations. The primary questions it must answer are not "How much?" or "By when?" but rather "For what?" and "Why?" What are the big issues or problems or opportunities that this institution addresses, and why are they important? Why is this institution unique and a worthy vehicle for addressing those matters? And, why is philanthropic support needed at this time?

Figure 4.1 includes an excerpt from some materials prepared for the Yale University campaign ("Yale Tomorrow: The Campaign for Yale University"), which demonstrates the construction of a well-stated case for support. (I have edited the statement from a longer message, obtained from the campaign website.) The statement summarizes the case for support of "the sciences," one priority in Yale's overall campaign. It begins with the big ideas—the historical contributions of science and the promise that science will continue to improve human life and society in this century. It then goes on to make the connection between those big ideas and Yale's capacity to have impact—its leading scientists, its location, and other characteristics that make it an attractive vehicle for advancing science. The summary then explains why support is needed—"to help keep the best minds working here and equip them to make the discoveries that will benefit humankind tomorrow." Finally, it concludes by returning to the larger purpose and offering donors an opportunity to have a "timely effect on the wider world we aspire to serve" (Yale University, 2009).

Yale's statement succinctly answers the questions "For what larger purpose?" "Why this institution?" and "Why philanthropy now?" Constructing the case in this logical way is essential in order to give the case both an intellectual and emotional appeal, or, as consultant Harold J. Seymour wrote, "to catch the eye, warm the heart, and stir the mind" (Seymour, 1966, p. 22).

An institution's needs, especially as they may be perceived by those who work on campus, are not compelling to donors unless linked to larger ideas. For example, small faculty offices, inadequate study space for students, and outdated athletic facilities may be annoyances to the people who must face them every day, and they may indeed impede education. But they are by themselves inadequate reasons for donors to sacrifice. Donors are inspired by the principles and ideals the institution represents, its vision

---

THE SCIENCES

Scientific method has yielded progressively deeper insights about the nature of our world since its introduction in the seventeenth century. Reasoned discovery has supplanted superstition, and at key moments—from the industrial revolution to the information age—new knowledge and its applications have transformed people's attitudes and livelihoods. . . .

In the twenty-first century, scientists around the world will have a massive impact on society, thanks to an explosion of new knowledge in biology and other fields—and better ways to use it. Computers let us model complex systems so that we can reliably test hypotheses at vastly accelerated speeds. We have the ability to image and manipulate matter at extreme scales, probing the far edges of the universe and the atom-by-atom assembly of materials. And where certain disciplines meet—like cell biology and clinical medicine or chemistry and energy research—today's science promises major leaps forward. . . .

At Yale, we have participated for decades in scientific advances that drive America's health and prosperity. Our faculty is home to leading thinkers in fields from genetics to quantum computing and from biomedical engineering to nanoscience. On our medical campus, researchers and physicians break new ground every day in the treatment of cancer, neurological disorders, and cardiovascular disease. And in New Haven and its environs, Yale discoveries have launched a thriving biotechnology industry. In short, we are prepared as few institutions are to advance basic knowledge and to apply it to today's greatest challenges. . . .

Your gifts to the Yale Tomorrow campaign can help keep the best minds working here and equip them to make the discoveries that will benefit humankind tomorrow. Science education, research, or clinical medicine—wherever you direct your gift, you can have a lasting impact on the University and a timely effect on the wider world we aspire to serve.

SOURCE: Yale University. (2009). "The Sciences: A Message from the President." yaletomorrow.yale.edu/priorities/sciences.html (accessed June 6, 2009; condensed by the author from a longer statement).

Figure 4.1.   Yale Tomorrow: The Campaign for Yale University

for the future, and the potential of its impact on lives, including their own, and on humanity.

Some browsing of the Web reveals cases for support that seem to be built around an institution's niche in the marketplace; they are focused on the need to increase endowment or improve facilities to match those of competitors. It is reasonable to wonder how compelling that approach may be to prospective donors. Alumni may feel the excitement of athletic competition with a rival college or university, but do they really respond to data showing that the alumni participation rate at their college or university is lower than that of others or that its endowment is less than that of market basket institutions? Unless such data are presented in the right context, they may be unlikely to motivate significant gifts. Indeed, the data may send a negative message, that is, they may demonstrate to alumni who do not give that others do not either. People respond with gifts when there are crises, such as natural disasters; but with regard to colleges and universities, people respond more to positive opportunities than to weaknesses or competitive threats.

A good case is one that is authentic. That is, the vision of the institution's future that is described must be believable. Ambitions such as "joining the ranks of America's great research universities" or "preparing society's leaders for the next century" may be appropriate for some colleges and universities, although they are not exactly original phrases. But for other institutions, such goals are just not realistic and thus do not ring true. Big ideas do attract the interest of donors, but exaggerated statements may sound like puffery. Not every gift or campaign is "transformational" and the term may be over-used. As John Ford, senior vice president at Stanford, explains, "Universities evolve." He continues, "'Transformation' conveys a 'once in a lifetime' leap, but we make big changes more than once. . . . There are constant efforts to do better, sometimes with bold strokes and some over time. I've seen both in the same campaign" (Shea, 2008).

A good case is one that builds on an institution's genuine strengths. For some, having an impact on the economic and cultural life of a community or state, helping students of disadvantaged backgrounds achieve success, advancing the standards of a specific profession or industry, or sustaining a particular educational philosophy are important and appropriate purposes.

I think, for example, of one public university that I assisted with planning for its campaign. Historically, many of its alumni had pursued teaching careers and, indeed, were represented in schools at all levels throughout the state. The president of the university spoke eloquently about that tradition and the contribution of the university's graduates to generations of young people as well as their communities and the economy of the region. She expressed no hyperbolic ambitions for global impact, but the case she made was compelling and moving. It was authentic, it was real. The nation does not need four thousand Harvards, and not all donors may believe that to be a desirable or plausible objective for their college or university.

PRINCIPLES OF THE GIFT RANGE CHART

The caliber of the institution's prospect pool, the dollar goals of the campaign, and the campaign's objectives—the purposes for which the funds are being raised—are interrelated. A realistic goal reflects the financial capacity and commitment of its prospects, but the latter will depend in part on the priorities and objectives of the campaign. Donors who do have financial capacity may be willing to stretch for some purposes but not for others; for example, they may give to cure cancer but not to improve campus landscaping. The objectives that are included in the campaign also must make sense in terms of a realistic dollar goal. In other words, the institution may not have the prospects to support all of its objectives and some may need to be accomplished, at least in part, through other sources of funding. This is often true of building projects, which may cost much more than can be expected from the campaign and will require debt financing as well as fundraising. (There are important requirements related to the use of debt financing that are not discussed in this book, but which need careful attention.) Sorting out all of this is the work of campaign planning. The gift range chart is a powerful tool that can anchor analysis and decision making throughout that process.

The gift range chart is also sometimes called a gift standards chart or just a gift chart. I have always thought that the format in which it is presented is more accurately a table, but it is usually called a chart and that term is used in this book.

Many people are familiar with the gift range chart, but not all may appreciate the full extent of its usefulness and power. It is an invaluable tool in planning the campaign, in management of the campaign throughout its duration, and for post-campaign analysis.

The principles that underlie the gift range chart reflect the observations of practitioners over the years in successful campaigns. That is, it depicts historical patterns of giving that have occurred in such efforts. Because the patterns are somewhat consistent from campaign to campaign, the chart can also be developed prospectively as a planning tool. In other words, a given campaign goal *requires* a distribution of gifts that generally coincides with the proportions of the gift range chart, and developing the chart may be one of the first steps in planning. The requirements of the chart can be compared with the institution's pool of prospects for a preliminary assessment of whether a suggested goal may be realistic. The gift range chart is thus a kind of theory. Grounded in observation, it has predictive power. But fundraising is art as well as science and it is not assured that the results of one or even many experiments will be replicated in a specific case. Fortunately, the gift range chart is a flexible tool that can be adapted to varied assumptions and circumstances.

Table 4.1 includes a gift range chart for a hypothetical campaign with a goal of $250 million. *It reflects traditional assumptions that may not be realistic in today's world*, as will be explained. But it nevertheless provides a starting point for discussion.

The principal assumptions reflected in the traditional gift range chart are (1) a lead gift equivalent to 10 percent of the goal; (2) the 80/20 rule (also called the Pareto Principle); and (3) the rule of thirds. The Pareto Principle is named for the economist Vilfredo Pareto, who observed that 20 percent of effort accounts for 80 percent of results in many endeavors, including commercial business. Translated to fundraising, the rule suggests that 80 percent of gifts will come from just 20 percent of donors, and the traditional gift range chart reflects that ratio. The rule of thirds is attributed to Harold J. Seymour, who observed that in most campaigns, about one-third of the total came from the top ten gifts, another third came from the next one hundred largest gifts, and the balance from all other gifts (Seymour, 1966).

But many experts say that these traditional guidelines are obsolete, for several reasons. For one, the 80/20 rule and the rule of thirds does not describe the actual patterns of giving seen in recently completed campaigns. In the boom years of the late 1990s, as well as in the mid-2000s, many campaigns were receiving as much as 90–95 percent of gifts from just 5–10 percent of donors. In other words, a relatively small number of large gifts has accounted for an increasing percentage of total dollars raised.

A study by the consulting firm Grenzebach Glier and Associates cited the striking example of the University of Virginia's $3 billion campaign, in which 1 percent of donors had given 80 percent of the funds raised, and offered data to suggest that the 80/20 rule has long been obsolete. The firm's analysis of all gifts over the entire lifetime of selected nonprofit organizations and institutions found that 20 percent of donors gave 90 percent of all support received. At colleges and universities, 80 percent of total support came from 2–3.5 percent of donors. The authors of a report on the study characterize the situation as "half-full/half-empty." Additional effort by just a few donors could change campaign results significantly, but the concentration of support also means that an institution can be vulnerable if its top donors should lose interest (Grenzebach Glier and Associates, 2008).

Another study, conducted in 2007 by the Council for Advancement and Support of Education (CASE) and the consulting firm Alexander Haas Martin & Partners, challenged the rule of thirds, but also noted different patterns depending on the goal of the campaign. The top ten gifts accounted for 46.7 percent of the goal in campaigns with goals of up to $100 million, but just 22 percent in campaigns with goals of $1 billion or more (Strout, 2007, p. A22). Those findings are understandable. Most $1 billion or higher goals are at universities. In a comprehensive campaign at a research university, annual giving from a large alumni base and grants from foundations and corporations for research and programs would be expected to comprise a significant portion of the total dollars raised in a campaign. In this situation, the top ten gifts then might account for a smaller percentage of the overall total. But a college with a smaller constituency and not so much support from foundations and corporations would need to obtain a much higher percentage of the overall campaign goal from a small number of leadership gifts.

In view of changing patterns in campaign giving, in 2003 Robert Pierpont offered a new formulation of Seymour's rule of thirds, reflecting a greater dependence on top gifts and bringing the dimensions of the traditional gift range chart more into alignment with contemporary experience (Pierpont, 2003, p. 126):

- About 40 to 60 percent of the goal should come from the ten to fifteen largest gifts.
- About 33 to 50 percent should come from the next 100 to 150 gifts.
- About 10 to 20 percent of the goal should come from all other gifts.

Whether the demise of the traditional standards reflects the economic booms of the 1990s and mid-2000s and whether giving will return to more traditional patterns in the future is, of course, impossible to know from today's vantage point. The growing importance of the top gifts in campaigns has coincided with unprecedented creation of new wealth and increasing disparities in wealth within society in the past two decades. It is possible to believe that the 1990s and 2000s were unique periods and that patterns of wealth and giving may shift toward those that have been more typical historically.

Speaking at a 2009 conference of CASE, Bruce McClintock, chairman of the consulting firm Marts & Lundy, argued that indeed the number of gifts of $5 million and above was likely to decline as a result of anticipated slower growth in the economy and asset values. He predicted that the total raised from the top 1 percent of donors would shrink from 70 percent of dollars to 50 percent in the years after 2009. He also predicted that the middle ranges, generally gifts of $100,000 to $999,999, which accounted for 4 percent of donors and 25 percent of dollars in the mid-2000s, could in the future encompass 9 percent of donors giving 40 percent of the campaign total. And the bottom ranges, which have accounted for 5 percent of dollars and 95 percent of donors in recent campaigns, could come to account for 10 percent of gift totals and 90 percent of donors. McClintock suggested that colleges and universities might need to shift their attention from the very top levels of the gift range chart to the middle and, indeed, to the annual fund gifts at the bottom (Masterson, 2009).

If McClintock is right, there are clear implications for the design of campaigns and for the allocation of fundraising staff and resources. Perhaps Pareto (of the 80/20 rule) will make a comeback. There could also be a renewed emphasis on building alumni relations programs and developing broad-based annual giving. But the future of annual giving is also uncertain. Some interpret the decline in alumni annual fund participation in recent decades as a trend that may work against broad-based giving and maintain, or even increase, higher education's reliance on the big gifts at the top of the chart.

There are gift range calculator tools available on the Web, for example, one offered by the software company Blackbaud (Blackbaud, 2009). Such calculators produce a gift range chart that is mathematically generated. It begins with a 10 percent lead gift. The level of gift at each successive level of the chart is then reduced by one-half, and the number of donors at each lower gift level is about doubled. That purely mathematical approach produces some unusual numbers; for example, Blackbaud's chart for a $250 million campaign calls for a 10 percent lead gift of $25 million, two gifts of $12.5 million, and five gifts of $6,250,000. A chart generated in this way would require some manipulation to be a good fit for a specific campaign, to present the round numbers that most donors are accustomed to seeing, and to match gifts in the chart with specific naming opportunities.

Whether planning begins with a traditional gift range chart, one reflecting more contemporary patterns, or one that is mathematically generated, it is likely that the chart will need to be manipulated to fit the specific situation. Patterns of giving—both anticipated and realized—will vary depending upon the size of the overall campaign, its priorities, and the size and capacity of the institution's constituency, among other variables.

There are several practical reasons why an institution might depart from standard gift-chart assumptions. For example, suppose that a lead gift exceeding 10 percent of the goal is anticipated, perhaps from an especially capable and committed board member or campaign leader. It would be foolish to ever present a gift range chart with a top gift at just 10 percent; the top gift shown should be whatever is expected from that donor, with other levels of the chart to be adjusted accordingly.

An institution with a fairly small constituency will likely need to proceed with a very top-loaded chart, that is, it will need to rely on a small number of large gifts toward the top of the chart given by just a few donors; it might need a top gift of 20 percent or even more. Institutions with a larger number of prospects may be able to obtain their goals with more gifts in the middle ranges, and more in lower ranges as a result of robust annual giving. But that is not to suggest that smaller gifts can make up for the absence of gifts at or near the top ranges. It is sometimes possible to reach the goal without the top gift, but only if there are a significant number of major gifts at the levels just below it. Relying on a broad base to compensate for the absence of major gifts (for example, the old idea of raising $1 million with $1,000 gifts from one thousand people) is a formula for failure in higher education campaigns, for reasons that have been discussed already.

The number of gifts at various levels in the gift range chart also may need to be adjusted to coincide with objectives of the campaign and donor-recognition opportunities. For example, if an objective of the campaign is to obtain endowments for ten professorships, each endowed at $2.5 million, the chart should show at least ten gifts at that level. If a new building has two wings that each can be named for a gift of $5 million, then the chart needs to show at least two gifts at $5 million. Inconsistency between the gift range chart and the list of recognition opportunities at various levels may cause confusion and the appearance of poor planning. Achieving such consistency may drive the gift range chart away from traditional assumptions and purely mathematical proportions. That is fine, so long as it follows the general principles previously discussed.

Finally, the length of the campaign influences the gift range chart. For example, if a campaign encompasses seven or eight years of annual giving and grant support, the top ten gifts will likely account for a smaller percentage of the overall total than if the campaign runs for just five years— there would be more of the campaign coming from the smaller gifts toward the bottom of the chart.

EVALUATING THE PROSPECT POOL

The gift range chart can be used as a tool for making a preliminary assessment of a proposed campaign goal. That assessment can be sobering. There may be instances in which some board members or others suggest a campaign goal without a realistic judgment about the fundraising capacity of the college or university. Or the needs and ambitions of various academic units and programs may add up to a large number, and there is internal pressure on the president to raise enough to meet them all. Developing a gift range chart based on the suggested goal and comparing its requirements to the institution's prospect pool can bring reality to bear on such discussions. A president who is confronted with the suggestion of an ambitious goal is wise to suggest some preliminary planning and then return to a follow-up discussion with a gift range chart in hand. Boards presented with a proposed campaign by the president or the chief development officer also should request such further analysis before proceeding. A gift range chart combined with an analysis of the prospect pool grounds such discussion in specific questions: "What gifts will be needed?" "How many?" and "From whom might they come?"

There are various opinions among experts on exactly what conversion ratio to anticipate in the gift range chart, that is, how many prospects are needed at each level in order to produce the number of gifts required in each range to achieve the campaign goal. Historically, the ratio was assumed to be about 3:1. Many today argue for a ratio of 5:1, and others suggest that the table be constructed with different ratios across the ranges. But the right ratio depends in part on what is known about the prospects, that is, the amount of confidence that the institution has in its ratings of them.

There are, of course, two principal elements to the rating of any prospect. The first is financial capacity, that is, the ability of the prospect to make a gift at the indicated level. The second variable is some measure of the probability that the prospect will be motivated to make a gift to the particular institution in response to the proposed priorities and objectives of the campaign. This variable is defined in different ways and may be called interest, commitment, inclination, readiness, or something else. The idea is somewhat like the concept of expected value in mathematics; that is, a value multiplied by the probability of its occurrence. In other words, a prospect capable of giving $100,000 with a 50 percent probability of doing so would be "expected" to produce $50,000. But of course, that is a hypothetical number; the approach may be useful in the aggregate across a large number of prospects, but may not be meaningful in a specific case, which may produce a gift of $100,000, something less, or zero.

If prospects are well known and highly cultivated, that is, if their capacity and inclination can be estimated with confidence, fewer may be needed to produce the required gifts because the conversion ratio, or closure rate, will be high. If financial capacity is uncertain or if the prospects have not been well cultivated, then a higher number will be needed to produce a gift, that is, the conversion ratio will be lower.

Some think that a higher ratio may be needed in the upper ranges of the gift range chart than in lower ones, since some of the prospects solicited at higher levels will actually give at lower levels, filling in some of the spaces on those rungs. And, of course, a larger gift is a more significant decision for a donor to reach. But others argue that a lower ratio is acceptable at higher levels, since the prospects for top gifts are likely to be among the best known to the institution's leaders, and thus their ratings are more reliable. Those people might argue that a higher ratio is indeed appropriate in lower gift ranges, because many of the prospects who are rated at those levels may be less well known and cultivated. For simplicity, table 4.1 uses a ratio of 4:1 throughout.

Again, there is no one right answer to the question of how many prospects are required at each level to produce a gift at that level. It depends on how much information the institution has available and on the reliability of that information. But there is no room for wishful thinking, and ratings need to be carefully evaluated.

Table 4.1. Gift Range Chart

Goal of $250 Million

Gift Range	No. of Gifts Required	No. of Prospects Required	Total at This Level	Cumulative Total	Cumulative Percentage of Goal
Top Ten Gifts:					
$25,000,000	1	4	$25,000,000	$25,000,000	10%
10,000,000	3	12	30,000,000	55,000,000	22%
5,000,000	6	24	30,000,000	85,000,000	34%
Next 100 Gifts:					
2,500,000	12	48	30,000,000	115,000,000	46%
1,000,000	27	108	27,000,000	142,000,000	57%
500,000	52	208	26,000,000	168,000,000	67%
Balance of Gifts:					
250,000	100	400	25,000,000	193,000,000	77%
100,000	180	720	18,000,000	211,000,000	84%
50,000	300	1,200	15,000,000	226,000,000	90%
25,000	560	2,240	14,000,000	240,000,000	96%
<25,000	Many	Many	10,000,000	$250,000,000	100%
TOTALS	1,241+	4,964+	$250,000,000	NA	NA

NOTE: Chart follows traditional "rule of thirds." Chart displays 4:1 conversion ratio.

A full discussion of prospect research is beyond the scope of this book. Presidents and other senior leaders need know only enough about research methods to ask appropriate questions in order to make a judgment about the quality of the data on which they will make decisions about campaign goals and objectives. Electronic screening of the database, a service provided by a number of vendors, may be especially helpful to an institution with a large constituency. Such programs access public information to produce a rating for each prospect in the database and identify, at least as a first cut, prospects worthy of more detailed research.

Screening and rating of prospects by volunteers is a traditional method that may still be effective in the right circumstances. For example, if a college's constituency is primarily in one community where people know something about each other's circumstances, peer screening and rating may provide better insight than electronic screening, at lower cost, and include more soft information about prospects' attitudes, family situations, and other relevant variables that electronic screening may not reveal. Colleges that have a tradition of strong class identity and active alumni chapters also may find that involving volunteers in the rating of donor prospects is an effective approach, which also has the benefit of engaging those volunteers in thinking about their own role in the campaign. But peer screening and rating may be less helpful in other settings, for example, among alumni of a large public university at which few students knew their classmates. Ratings of prospects by development officers always need to be viewed carefully. On the one hand, a rating by a professional who has met the prospect may be more credible than one developed through public information. But on the other hand, development professionals are by nature optimistic people.

A feasibility study or market survey, whether conducted by an external consultant or institutional staff, also may provide additional information that adds confidence to prospect ratings. That subject will be discussed further.

SETTING CAMPAIGN GOALS

Setting the dollar goal of a campaign is, of course, one of the critical decisions that the campaign leadership faces. As discussed previously, a preliminary or working goal may be established early in planning. The goal may be revised upward or downward following further prospect research or a feasibility study and again as the quiet phase of the campaign unfolds and the size of the nucleus fund that can be produced becomes more clear. The goal that is announced at the kickoff may be higher or lower than the preliminary goal determined months or years before, but again, it is usually

best to manage expectations and to keep the discussion of preannouncement goals within reasonable bounds; it is better to go up than down.

The dollar goal of the campaign, and possibly subgoals for specific academic units, programs, or priorities, should be data driven. They should reflect an assessment of the prospect pool *against* the priorities and objectives
of the campaign. In reality, of course, other factors may come to influence
the discussion. Some may simply look to a campaign at another institution and argue that "if they can do it, so can we." Or, they may just go for
a number that sounds impressive. That happened at one university that
I advised in its campaign planning. The institution's previous campaign
had raised about $50 million, and my careful analysis suggested that its
next campaign might achieve a goal of $70–80 million. I recommended a
preliminary goal of $70 million, knowing that some would likely push for
a higher figure, hopefully remaining within the range that I thought to be
achievable. At the meeting at which my recommendation was presented,
one otherwise thoughtful trustee strongly made the case for setting the goal
at $100 million, to coincide with the one hundredth anniversary of the in-
stitution, which would be celebrated near the end of the campaign. It was
a suggestion based on the assumption that donors respond to dollar goals
rather than the objectives of the campaign, or to goals based on unrelated
milestones, such as anniversaries.

In this case, fortunately, more rational heads prevailed and the president
was steadfast. The preliminary goal was set at $75 million, within the range
that I had recommended, and the more ambitious trustee was satisfied with
the idea that the goal could be increased before announcement if the quiet
phase of the campaign went especially well. Of course, perhaps without
realizing, his advocacy of the higher goal also had focused attention on his
own commitment to the nucleus fund. (This is a real case, although I have
changed the numbers slightly in order to fully disguise the institution and
its trustee.)

A data-driven approach to setting the campaign goal would include
matching the prospects required at each level of the gift range table with
an analysis of the institution's prospect pool and answering the simple
question, Do we have the prospects needed to produce the gifts required
to achieve the proposed goal, given typical conversion ratios? But in many
campaigns, the situation is somewhat more complicated. In a comprehensive campaign, the annual fund may comprise a substantial component of
the overall campaign goal. Projecting the total of annual giving over the
years of the campaign may rely on past experience and historical ratios as
well as prospect ratings. In campaigns at universities that include research
and program grants in their comprehensive campaigns, projecting such
revenue over a period of several years may be difficult, since so much depends on faculty initiatives and the changing priorities of funders. The rate

at which bequests may be realized over the course of the campaign is obviously difficult to project, although again, past experience may be a guide if the college or university has an ongoing planned giving program. The campaign plan may anticipate that bequest expectancies will be credited toward the overall goal. If so, the standards by which they are counted will affect the total anticipated from this source as a portion of the campaign total. Campaign counting standards are discussed again in chapter 5.

Setting the campaign goal involves art as well as science. It is best not to go too far beyond what the analysis of data suggests to be realistic, but great achievements are never built on totally safe numbers. Inevitably there will be an x-factor of institutional aspiration that must be added to the campaign total of which the institution is confident, in order to establish a goal that is ambitious and exciting. And while no responsible expert endorses establishing a campaign goal merely to match or exceed that of another institution, it is a reality that campaigns are in part a positioning strategy for the institution. Colleges and universities do carefully watch one another's campaigns and consider them in their own campaign planning. One reason why standards in reporting campaign totals are important is to assure that benchmarking compares apples to apples and not to some other type of fruit. The latter method may lead a college or university down a path that inevitably ends in disappointment.

Achieving the right balance between safe goals and wild fantasies requires judgment. Weighing the risks of failure against the need to generate excitement, challenge the board and donors, and send the right message about the institution's future requires wisdom. Both are essential components of the president's responsibility for leadership.

DEFINING CAMPAIGN PRIORITIES AND OBJECTIVES

In addition to dollar goals, campaigns—by definition—address specific purposes that reflect priorities of the institution. Defining these purposes is a critical task in campaign planning.

The vocabulary of campaigns has evolved over time and some terms are used inconsistently, both among authors and campaigns. That is not necessarily a problem, so long as everyone involved understands what they mean in a specific context, but some further clarity might be helpful.

The terms "goal" and "goals" are used fairly consistently and refer to the dollar totals that the campaign is expected to achieve. There may be an overall goal and then various subgoals, which may be broken out in various ways, as discussed shortly.

But the *purposes* for which the dollars are being raised have come to be described and presented in different ways over time. In earlier decades they were usually called "needs," and a compilation of them was the "needs list." The term has somewhat of a charitable connotation, and it reflects an internal perspective, but "needs" is still used in some campaigns and in conversations about them.

In the 1990s, the purposes of campaigns came to be identified as "objectives," adopting some of the language and perspective of strategic planning. Some were sometimes highlighted as "featured objectives," that is, the objectives receiving the most emphasis. Objectives are similar to needs, that is, they are specific purposes such as endowment for chairs or scholarships or construction or renovation of buildings. Both terms—objectives and featured objectives—are still widely used to describe the purposes of campaigns.

In the 2000s, there has been a trend toward identifying campaign "priorities" or "strategic priorities," under which objectives are often organized. These are broad, cross-cutting themes that place the campaign in the context of the institution's overall strategy and direction. Some campaign priorities reflect external themes (e.g., "preserving the environment," "advancing medical knowledge") and some describe priorities that are more campus focused (e.g., "advancing undergraduate education," "strengthening faculty research"). Some campaigns abbreviate the latter and organize campaign goals simply around the priorities of "students," "faculty," and so forth.

The terms "priorities" and "objectives" are not consistently applied within the field. Some campaigns use the terms interchangeably. Some nest objectives within priorities and some priorities within objectives. Again, that is not necessarily a problem, so long as there is consistency within a particular campaign.

The goals of a comprehensive campaign can be sliced in five basic ways:

1. *By the use of the funds*—endowment, capital projects (facilities and equipment), and current use (both unrestricted and restricted). By definition, comprehensive campaigns encompass giving for all of these uses. Gifts as well as pledges and, in many cases, planned gift commitments, will be credited toward one or another, and some donors will combine the annual fund, an endowment gift, and perhaps support for a building project within a single commitment to the campaign.

2. *By priorities.* As an example, there may be a subgoal of the campaign related to the priority of advancing undergraduate education, which subsumes current scholarship support as well as endowment objectives and some facilities projects, perhaps construction or renovation or a student center or residence halls—projects related to the undergraduate experience. A priority of advancing knowledge might encompass endowed chairs and professorships as well as funds for research, laboratories, or libraries.

3. *By unit*, including colleges and schools, research institutes or centers, and campus-wide programs such as athletics or student life. In universities, defining goals and objectives for each major unit helps to harness the leadership of deans and the loyalty that many alumni attach to the college or school from which they received their educations. In many comprehensive campaigns, each component of the overall effort operates like a campaign of its own, with volunteer leadership, development staff, and deans carrying out all of the roles described in chapter 3, with overall coordination and direction, more or less, from the central administration.

4. *By objectives.* Some smaller campaigns do not describe cross-cutting themes or priorities. Rather, they go right to specific projects, for example, $10 million for endowed scholarships and $10 million for renovation of the student center.

5. *By the impact of commitments.* CASE's campaign management guidelines encourage institutions to break out the overall campaign goal into separate goals for current and deferred gifts and to maintain this distinction in reporting campaign progress. This helps to avoid misunderstanding about the impact of campaign commitments, some of which may be available to the institution immediately and some of which may become available only in the future (*CASE Reporting Standards and Management Guidelines*, 2009).

Institutions adopt different formats for displaying the goals and purposes of their campaigns. That is acceptable, but it is important to maintain clarity and simplicity. The goals, priorities, and objectives of a well-planned campaign should be consistent when viewed from various perspectives. In other words, they should form a matrix in which the cross-cutting priorities can be spread across academic units or the use of funds with a number in each cell and consistent totals for each row and column.

As one example, table 4.2 summarizes goals of "Beyond Boundaries: The Campaign for Tufts," a $1.2 billion campaign. The goals are summarized on the university's website by purpose (what was called "use" earlier), by priorities, and by academic unit. Drilling down into one of the priorities or into one of the academic units reveals further detail on the campaign.

The $333 million goal for the priority of "fostering an outstanding faculty" cuts across the use of funds. It includes endowed professorships, as well as expendable funds for faculty recruitment and development initiatives and other current purposes, and start-up costs for laboratories (capital).

Table 4.2 shows the breakdown of the $100 million goal for one of Tufts's academic units, the Fletcher School. The $100 million encompasses

$44.5 million for student aid, $42 million for faculty and research, $6.5 million for building renovation, and $7.0 million for the annual fund. Those are objectives; they derive from the university-wide priorities and include funds for current use, endowment, and capital.

Table 4.3 offers another example and a somewhat different approach, from Bowdoin College's simply named "The Bowdoin Campaign." The overall campaign goal of $250 million is broken out into college-wide priorities (which some might call objectives), including financial aid, academic affairs, annual giving, student affairs, and building projects. Looking inside one of the boxes reveals more detail. For example, the academic affairs goal of $69.5 million is organized by priorities and objectives within each of those priorities. So, "enrichment of academic programs" (goal $37.5 million) includes $35 million for faculty positions (endowment), $2 million as a "bridge for endowed positions" (current support), and $500,000 for "new curriculum funding" (current support). As Table 4.3 shows, Bowdoin uses footnotes to indicate the use of funds, where (e) equals endowment, (s) means spendable, and (r) refers to renovation projects. As a college, Bowdoin does not need to present its campaign goals by academic unit in the way that a university might.

Table 4.4 provides a third example, from Princeton University's $1.75 billion campaign ("Aspire: A Plan for Princeton"). Using a somewhat different vocabulary, but a familiar format, Princeton presents a "table of needs" in which the overall goal is divided among six "strategic areas." The strategic areas are similar to what others might call "priorities"—they are cross-cutting and include both larger and campus-specific themes. On the campaign website, clicking on one of the priorities leads to a fuller description. For example, "engineering and a sustainable society" offers descriptions of programs that are interdisciplinary and that cut across Princeton schools, including the Woodrow Wilson School, the School of Engineering and Applied Science, and the Princeton Environmental Institute. The objectives described under this priority also cut across the use of funds and include current program support as well as a new facility for the engineering school.

It is only realistic to acknowledge, again, that there is some art involved in the definition of campaign goals, priorities, and objectives. In addition to the priorities established through academic planning, there also may be known donor preferences that must be acknowledged. Some may have interests that lie in one or another school, department, or program, and their gifts will be forthcoming only if those units are sufficiently represented in the priorities of the campaign. There may be prospects whose main interest is in a particular building project, perhaps the renovation of a building already named for their family or central to the agenda of the school from which they graduated. At universities with medical centers, some prospects

Table 4.2.   Beyond the Boundaries: The Campaign for Tufts

Campaign Overall Goal: $1.2 Billion
Goals by Purpose (Use)

Endowment	60%
Capital	21%
Current Use	19%

Goals by Priorities

Supporting the Student Experience	$380 million
Fostering an Outstanding Faculty	$333 million
Building and Enhancing the Physical Infrastructure	$277 million
Supporting Academic Innovation	$127 million
Annual Support for Current Initiatives	$83 million
Total	$1.2 billion

Fostering an Outstanding Faculty
(Goal: $333 million)

Each school at Tufts University is challenged by intense competition for the next generation of scholar-teachers. Underwriting endowed professorships (*endowment*), and supporting diverse faculty recruitment and development initiatives (*current use*), will bolster resources that will help the university attract, retain, and support the world's leading teachers, scholars, and scientists. In addition, this priority will help Tufts meet start-up costs associated with attracting top-notch scientists who require appropriate laboratory space (*capital*).

(Terms in italics added by author).

will be particularly interested in research on diseases that have affected their own families or the research of a physician who treated them. And, of course, members of the board or the campaign planning committee may have preferences that will be reflected in the decisions ultimately made.

Even when campaign priorities are firmly rooted in an institution's strategic and academic plan, which priorities are emphasized in the campaign also need to reflect the realities of the philanthropic market. The campaign should be viewed as just one source of funding for implementing the institution's strategic plan, and other sources may also need to be part of the larger implementation program. Some things are just more attractive to

Table 4.2. cont. Beyond the Boundaries: The Campaign for Tufts

Goals by Unit

School of Arts and Sciences	$425 million
School of Engineering	$150 million
School of Medicine	$225 million
Tisch College of Citizenship and Public Service	$60 million
School of Dental Medicine	$40 million
The Fletcher School	$100 million
Friedman School of Nutrition Science and Policy	$50 million
Cummings School of Veterinary Medicine	$100 million
Cross-University Initiatives	$50 million
Total	$1.2 billion

The Fletcher School
(Goal: $100 Million)

Student Aid	$44.5 million
Faculty and Research	$42 million
Building Renovation	$6.5 million
Annual Fund	$7.0 million
Total	$100 million

SOURCE: Tufts University. (2009). "Campaign Priorities." giving.tufts.edu/campaign/priorities.html (accessed May 11, 2009).

donors than others, and it makes little sense to load up the campaign with priorities and objectives that no one will support.

Early in my tenure as director of development at the University of Maryland–College Park, in about 1977, I was visited by the young chairman of the math department. He had come to talk with me about how to raise money for his department. I was young, too, and had not fully developed my diplomatic skills. I just told him it was just impossible to raise money for the math department. He accepted my judgment with courtesy and we became friends. He also proceeded to prove me wrong.

In the years that followed, he went on to become one of the outstanding leaders in higher education, serving as president at Maryland, president at

Table 4.3. Bowdoin College: The Bowdoin Campaign

Overall Goal $250 Million	
Overall Campaign Priorities	
Financial Aid	$76.55 million (31%)
⌐ Academic Affairs	$69.5 million (28%)
Annual Giving	$43.1 million (17%)
Student Affairs	$32.75 million (13%)
Building Projects	$28.1 million (11%)
	$250 Million (100%)

Academic Affairs Priorities ($69.5 million: 28% of campaign goal)

Enrichment of Academic Program

Faculty positions (e)	$35,000,000
Bridge for endowed positions (s)	2,000,000
New curriculum funding (s)	500,000
	$37,500,000

Faculty Career Development

Enhanced sabbatical leave (e)	$9,000,000
Engagement with professional peers (e)	1,000,000
	$10,000,000

Enrichment of Intellectual Community

Coastal studies support (e)	$2,500,000
Environmental studies (e)	4,000,000
Bowdoin Scientific Statione	1,000,000
Symposia and visiting scholars (e)	2,500,000
	$10,000,000

Enhancement of Centers of Academic Excellence

Student research fellowships (e)	$2,000,000
Library resources (e)	2,000,000
Museum of Art (e)	2,000,000
Educational Technology Program (e)	1,000,000
Center for Teaching and Learning (e)	1,000,000
Curricular development funds (e)	1,000,000
	$9,000,000

Renovation of Academic Spaces (r)	$3,000,000
Total Academic Affairs	$69,500,000

(e) = endowment   (s) = spendable   (r) = renovation

SOURCE: Bowdoin College. (2009). "The Priorities." www.bowdoin.edu/support-bowdoin/campaign/priorities/index.shtml (accessed May 12, 2009).

Table 4.4. Aspire: A Plan for Princeton

Campaign Table of Needs	
Aspire: A Plan for Princeton encompasses the following six strategic areas:	
Annual Giving	$250 million
Engineering and a Sustainable Society	$325 million
Exploration in the Arts	$325 million
New Frontiers in Neuroscience	$300 million
Citizenship and the World	$300 million
The Princeton Experience	$250 million
TOTAL	$1.75B

SOURCE: The Trustees of Princeton University. (2009). "Campaign Table of Needs." giving.princeton.edu/goals/tableofneeds.xml (accessed June 16, 2009).

Ohio State, and then chancellor of the University of Maryland system, the position he now holds. I have always remembered that first meeting and have hoped as well that he does not.

The question of who influences the objectives of a campaign was examined in the Association of Governing Boards of Universities and Colleges' 2004 study of the board's role in fundraising, mentioned previously. The findings suggest that the philanthropic market is a consideration. The results of a 2004 survey were compared with those of a similar survey conducted by John Pocock in 1989. In both studies, chief advancement officers were asked to identify the four individuals or groups who had the most influence on setting campaign goals and objectives. Changes from 1989 to 2004 were evident. The most significant finding was the apparently diminished role of the chief academic officer and faculty committees. In 1989, 31.5 percent mentioned the chief academic officer as influential in setting campaign priorities, while that percentage declined to 3.1 percent in 2004. Faculty committees were mentioned by 30.2 percent in 1989 but just 2.3 percent in 2004 (Worth, 2005, p. 90).

There is an inevitable balance between the desire to raise funds against predetermined institutional priorities and accommodating the known interests and proclivities of donors. That is not to say that donors' preferences should drive institutional priorities, but in reality there is often a compromise between what the institution most prefers and what donors are willing to support.

Even when market realities are considered in setting campaign priorities, some are likely to receive more support than anticipated by the goal assigned to them, while others may remain underfunded at the conclusion of the campaign. The broad expanse of comprehensive campaigns and the long time periods they encompass make it impossible to project final results with precision. It is possible, indeed likely, that even if the overall campaign goal is met or exceeded, there will be remaining priorities that will need to be addressed in the post-campaign period. Some strategies for that period are discussed in chapter 8 of this book.

FEASIBILITY STUDY OR MARKET TEST

At the point in campaign planning where preliminary goals, priorities, objectives, and a pool of prospects have been defined, many institutions undertake some type of market test. This may be a feasibility study conducted by an outside consultant or a series of meetings, focus groups, and other activities undertaken by development staff. There are multiple benefits from such activity.

A feasibility study or other type of market test helps to gauge the reaction of key prospects to the institution's plans and messages and informs planning, possibly leading to a revision of the preliminary goals, priorities, objectives, and campaign plan. Second, it is the beginning of cultivation of those who are involved in interviews or discussion groups. This involvement may be the first step toward capturing their attention, stimulating their thinking about the institution and its goals, and providing them with an opportunity to help shape the effort in which they will eventually be asked to participate as a leader and/or donor.

The question of whether to engage an outside consultant for a campaign study or whether much of the market research can be undertaken by institutional staff is one that engenders debate. The term "feasibility study" originated in the days of the traditional capital campaign, which was usually focused on a specific building project. The purpose of the study was to determine whether the project was, literally, feasible. That is, the question was whether enough could be raised to cover most or all of the construction costs; if not, the project could not be undertaken or some alternative method of financing would need to be pursued. The institution needed to make financial commitments to the project and rely on gifts to cover them. There was a need for a high degree of confidence and precision in assessing the potential of raising money for the project.

In today's world of comprehensive campaigns, the question may not be whether to have a campaign. Rather, the questions are often more about when, for what, how much, and how. Accordingly, some consultants no longer use the term "feasibility study" and prefer "campaign planning study" as a more accurate description of the comprehensive service they provide. Such a study encompasses both internal data analysis and external interviews and informs campaign planning on such questions as timing and leadership, the relative attractiveness of various priorities, and broad questions about alternative campaign strategies, as well as dollar goals. But many people still refer to a pre-campaign study by a consultant simply as a feasibility study and are interested primarily in the recommended goal that the consultant provides.

Using a professional consultant for a feasibility or campaign planning study does offer advantages. A consultant brings expertise and broad experience in planning campaigns. Interviews may be especially informative and frank if conducted by someone who is objective and independent of the college or university. A consultant may bring authority and data to internal discussions of the campaign, either tempering unrealistic expectations or providing reassurance that an ambitious goal can be achieved.

As a matter of full disclosure, though, I must acknowledge that I have conducted campaign planning studies for a fee, so my opinion is not without bias. I believe that in many circumstances they add considerable value to an institution's campaign planning. But I also must reveal that I served as a director or vice president for development for over thirty years of my career and, in those positions, I planned and directed campaigns both with and without formal feasibility studies.

My opinion—based on a perspective from both sides of the transaction—is that the right answer depends entirely on the particular situation that an institution faces and its purposes in engaging a consultant. Sometimes a full-blown feasibility study is a very wise investment. At other times, a more limited and focused engagement of a consultant may be enough—perhaps he or she brings wisdom to the campaign planning committee's deliberations and helps to shape the campaign plan. Sometimes a consultant can provide a sounding board for the president, who may prefer to discuss sensitive campaign-related issues with someone objective from outside rather than members of the board or development staff. If the president and chief development officer are highly experienced in campaigns, if they have been at their institution for a long time, if the volunteer leaders of the campaign are experienced and wise, and if relationships with top prospects are well established, then a consultant may not be necessary at all. Those who say a consultant is always needed may be overselling. Those who argue that consultants are never needed may be overconfident.

Some type of market test, whether conducted by a consultant or staff, is a valuable exercise that informs the refinement of campaign goals, priorities, and plans as the institution moves toward the quiet phase and eventually to a public announcement. No corporation would launch a new product without some data about the market's probable response and, indeed, most product launches are preceded by extensive market surveys. Even if the senior leadership and top prospects for the campaign are well known and involved and a formal feasibility study is deemed unnecessary, it is still beneficial for the staff to discuss the campaign's proposed goals, priorities, and objectives with groups of alumni and other donor prospects—perhaps asking for input on drafts of the case statement and engaging people beyond the campus in campaign planning in other ways. Such discussions help to provide feedback to both development and communications planners and to prepare the way for the campaign's eventual reach into the institution's entire constituency.

This chapter has discussed some of the important decisions and tasks that need to be addressed during the campaign planning phase—defining the case; evaluating the institution's prospect pool; setting the campaign goal, priorities, and objectives; and completing a feasibility study or market test. But there are additional details that need attention during this phase; some are suggested by the list of readiness criteria with which this chapter began, including the campaign budget, systems, staffing, and policies regarding the acceptance and counting of gifts. Those topics will be explored in chapter 5.

REFERENCES

Blackbaud. (2009). "Gift Range Calculator." www.blackbaud.com/company/resources/giftrange/giftcalc.aspx (accessed June 15, 2009).

CASE Reporting Standards and Management Guidelines for Educational Fundraising. 4th edition. (2009). Washington, DC: Council for Advancement and Support of Education.

Dove, Kent E. (2000). *Conducting a Successful Capital Campaign.* 2nd edition. San Francisco: Jossey-Bass.

Grenzebach Glier and Associates. (2008). "80/20? An Outdated Basis for Planning" [electronic version]. *GG+A Quarterly Review,* Fall, p. 5. www.grenzebachglier.com/files/webfm/2008_Fall_ggqr.pdf (accessed June 15, 2009).

Masterson, Kathryn. (2009). "Colleges Will See Decline in Megagifts, Experts Predict" [electronic version]. *Chronicle of Higher Education,* July 13. chronicle.com/article/Colleges-Will-See-a-Decline/47371/(accessed July 29, 2009).

Pierpont, Robert. (2003). "Capital Campaigns." In Henry A. Rosso & Associates, *Achieving Excellence in Fund Raising* (2nd edition), edited by Eugene A. Tempel. San Francisco: Jossey-Bass, Pp. 117–38.

Seymour, Harold J. (1966). *Designs for Fund-Raising: Principles, Patterns, and Techniques.* New York: McGraw-Hill.

Shea, Susan. (2008). "The Big Time" [electronic version]. *Currents,* April. www.case.org (accessed May 12, 2009).

Strout, Erin. (2007). "CASE Examines the Role of Big Gifts in Capital Campaigns." *Chronicle of Higher Education* 53, no. 46 (July 20), p. A22.

Voluntary Support of Education. (2008). New York: Council for Aid to Education.

Worth, Michael. (2005). *Securing the Future: A Fundraising Guide for Boards of Independent Colleges and Universities.* Washington, DC: Association of Governing Boards of Universities and Colleges.

Yale University. (2009). "The Sciences: A Message from the President." yaletomorrow.yale.edu/priorities/sciences.html (accessed June 6, 2009).

5

Campaign Resources and Policies

The previous chapter discussed some of the key tasks and decisions to be completed within the campaign's planning phase. This chapter continues the discussion of campaign planning with a focus on campaign budgeting and staffing and some policies that need to be in place before the campaign begins. The latter include those concerned with gift acceptance, donor recognition, and campaign counting and reporting.

BUDGETING FOR THE CAMPAIGN

The cost of a comprehensive campaign is, of course, a question that boards, presidents, and chief financial officers are likely to regard as quite important. Establishing the budget for the campaign is a critical element in the planning phase. It would be unrealistic to expect good returns without sufficient investment, but it is also reasonable to insist on efficiency and to establish standards of performance.

There is no universal or precise answer to the question of what budget is required for a campaign. Several variables affect it, including the scale of the institution's existing advancement or development program; the history of past campaigns, if any; the size of the anticipated goal; the geographic dispersion of prospects and the depth of existing relationships with them; the plan for solicitation (i.e., the relative importance of major gifts, the annual fund, grants); and the institution's nonfinancial goals for the campaign (for example, whether institutional visibility and branding are important purposes that will require a substantial investment in communication).

If a college or university has a long history of fundraising, established programs for annual and planned giving, well-developed information on its prospects, and an experienced and capable advancement staff, the cost of a campaign may be incremental, that is, it may require only augmentation of capacity that is already in place. For an institution beginning its first comprehensive campaign, there will be a need for substantial investment in research and systems, new staff appointments, consulting, and other resources. A campaign with a larger goal will require a larger budget than a smaller campaign will, although it may cost less in relative terms. There are some fixed costs that will not vary much by the size of the goal, for example, the development of campaign materials and consulting. Those costs are relatively smaller when amortized across a larger campaign.

If most prospects are within the institution's local community, state, or region, the campaign budget will require less for travel than if they are spread across the nation or the world. If prospects have been well cultivated and are ready to give, fewer contacts will be required to close gifts than if the prospects are less prepared. If the campaign will be focused on a relatively small number of leadership gift prospects, that is, the gift range chart is top loaded, fundraising may be more efficient than in a more broad-based effort. However, enhancing investment in the annual fund program may be nevertheless important, both to meet annual giving goals during the campaign and also to build a pipeline for future major gifts.

The campaign budget needs to be appropriately structured, that is, the funds need to be in the right lines. For example, filling the campaign office with dozens of major gift officers who have inadequate funds for travel would be unproductive. On the other hand, an army of gift officers does not guarantee a successful campaign if there are not well qualified prospects to engage. It might not be cost-effective for a college with relatively young alumni to invest in a sophisticated planned giving program, but additions to the annual fund staff might make sense. Hiring experienced foundation relations professionals is likely to be a sound investment for an institution that has programs consistent with foundation interests, but may not be the right area to emphasize for others. Some development offices allocate too little for positions that support front-line gift officers, for example, in the area of advancement services. The result is that well-compensated major gifts professionals spend too much time doing their own research, making appointments, arranging travel, and updating the database, detracting from their time spent with prospects and donors.

While there is no universal answer as to how much a campaign should cost and many variables to consider, there are some general guidelines that are often mentioned. They may provide the president and the board with an initial top-down ballpark within which to plan. Most experts estimate that the campaign budget should fall somewhere between 10 and 15 percent of the goal and all acknowledge that larger campaigns will be more cost-effective than smaller ones (see, for example, Dove, 2000; Gearhart, 2006; Kihlstedt, 2005). Some major university campaigns may cost as little as 4–5 percent and smaller campaigns may require expenses exceeding 15 percent of the goal. Dove (2000, p. 142) suggests that for a college or university with an already well-developed fundraising program, the incremental expenditure for a campaign, that is, the amount added to the ongoing budget for fundraising, may be about 4 percent of the campaign goal, but of course, that is a rough estimate and may not reflect at all the situation of any given college or university.

An institution that has a long history of fundraising and previous campaigns generally will fall lower in the range than an institution conducting its first or second campaign or that is significantly scaling up its fundraising efforts. But, some argue, the apparent lower cost of well-established programs ignores the substantial sunk costs of past activities in cultivating relationships with donors. Those relationships may mature within the current campaign but be attributable at least in part to expenditures made years before. Campaign cost accounting may not capture the full amount of the earlier investments. At the same time, investments in the current campaign will generate returns for years in the future and those returns—Cash's concept of post-campaign value, as discussed in chapter 1—also should be considered, although they may be difficult to measure.

Some experts suggest ranges for campaign expenditures by categories. For example, Andrea Kihlstedt (2005) estimates that about 55 percent of campaign expenditures will be for personnel; about 15 percent for office expenses, including travel and cultivation activities; about 25 percent for communications and public relations; and about 5 percent for various other expenses and contingencies. But those estimates may not be applicable to a campaign in which, for example, national and international travel may cost much more or for an institution without a long record of fundraising that will need to invest more in cultivation events.

There have been a number of studies of fundraising costs, including those undertaken by the Center on Philanthropy at Indiana University, the Association of Fundraising Professionals, and others. Most have looked at the nonprofit sector as a whole and have not focused on higher education or campaigns specifically. A study conducted by the Council for Advancement and Support of Education (CASE) and the National Association of College and University Business Officers in 1990 focused on costs of fundraising and other advancement functions in colleges and universities. It is generally known as the "Lilly study" in recognition of its funder, the Lilly Endowment (CASE, 1990). That study established the standards for fundraising cost accounting, but of course, the data are now out of date. In addition, the costs of fundraising may be different on an ongoing basis than during a campaign. An updated study of fundraising costs was launched by CASE in 2007 and was under way at the time of this writing. There are also a number of institutional consortia and peer groups that collect and share data that may be helpful to similar institutions.

It is important that boards and presidents view campaign expenditures as an *investment* rather than an expense. Historically, the ratio most commonly used to measure fundraising expense has been cost-per-dollar-raised, in other words, the percentage of the funds raised spent to raise them. For example, if an institution spends $5 million on fundraising and receives $50 million in gifts as a result, its cost would be 10 percent, but if the same expenditure brought in $100 million, its cost would be just 5 percent.

But that ratio or percentage is not the best metric to emphasize. It measures efficiency rather than effectiveness, that is, it focuses on cost rather than return on investment. If an institution spends even 50¢ to raise $1, which would be considered a very high fundraising cost, that would still represent a 100 percent return on its original investment. There are few investments that double, and a 100 percent return would be considered very good performance by the manager of an investment portfolio.

FINANCING THE CAMPAIGN

There are various methods for financing a campaign, for identifying the resources to pay for the staff and activity that the campaign requires. One way is to simply include the campaign, or some of it, as a line item in the institution's operating budget, the same as any other administrative function. There will be incremental costs that are specific to the campaign, for example, publications and events that may not be needed once the campaign has ended. But with campaigns lasting several years or more, many institutions find that the need for fundraising staff is not significantly reduced at the end of the campaign. While there may be turnover in the incumbents, many of the new positions created for a campaign may need to be maintained in order to manage ongoing major gifts fundraising, stewardship, and the natural growth of the program over the years—as well as to begin planning for the next campaign, which may come soon.

Thus, including at least some campaign staff positions in the regular operating budget of the institution may be a realistic approach if it is possible to do so. To the extent that the campaign helps to generate long-term increases in unrestricted giving, or produces budget-relieving gifts, there may be additional revenue to offset the added budget allocation.

Some institutions explicitly earmark unrestricted gifts to support the fundraising operation. There is no reason why such gifts cannot be used to meet fundraising expenses—unrestricted means unrestricted. But this approach can present some communication challenges and potentially some ethical concerns. If annual fund solicitation materials state that gifts are earmarked for fundraising, that may not be especially inspiring to donors. On the other hand, if annual fund materials state, or imply, that gifts are used for faculty or student support or academic purposes when they are indeed entirely earmarked for the fundraising budget, that is misleading and inappropriate. Another concern with the explicit use of annual fund gifts for the fundraising budget is that the development office leadership may become preoccupied with generating enough unrestricted revenue to cover its own costs, at the expense of focusing on major gifts that will have greater long-term impact on the college or university.

With careful budgeting and funds management, some restricted gifts may be budget relieving and thus as valuable as unrestricted support. For example, gifts to support current scholarships offset the needed allocation of institutional resources for student aid and thus may be as useful as unrestricted gifts. Endowed funds that are unrestricted or restricted for scholarships also add to flexible operating revenue in subsequent years. But tracking the budget impact of restricted gifts may be more complicated than most financial officers may think justified.

Independent colleges and universities generally have greater flexibility in how they pay for the campaign than do public institutions, which may face restrictions on the use of public money for fundraising. Institutions that face such restrictions may manage all of their fundraising through a related foundation, and the foundation must generate revenue to meet its own expenses. Institutions in that position use a variety of methods for generating campaign budget support. Some levy a charge against endowment income, an administrative services fee. Some charge what is commonly called a gift tax, that is, a percentage of gifts and/or bequests that is applied to operating expenses, including fundraising. Some use interest earned on the short-term investment of gift funds between the time of their receipt by the foundation and transfer to an institutional account for expenditure. Some independent institutions also use an endowment charge or some version of a gift tax to generate funds for a campaign.

It is essential to be forthright in communicating to donors what fees will be assessed on their gifts, especially gifts to endowment or for restricted current-use purposes. For endowment gifts, such charges are usually described in the gift agreement, which the donor and the institution sign. All such arrangements require both open communication and complete transparency.

CASE has developed an analysis of the pros and cons of common methods for funding foundations at public institutions, which applies as well to campaigns. It is available on the CASE website (www.case.org).

STAFFING THE CAMPAIGN

The management of a comprehensive campaign requires specialized professional skills and experience. And the campaign staff must be of appropriate size and configured in accordance with the goals and operational plan for the campaign.

If volunteers are highly engaged in the cultivation and solicitation of major gifts, that might seem to imply a need for fewer major gift officers on the development staff. However, as noted earlier in this book, volunteers are uncompensated but not free. They require training, support, management, and direction, and it is a mistake to not provide sufficient staffing for their efforts.

The gift range chart, discussed in chapter 4 of this book, provides one useful tool for estimating the professional staff needed for a campaign. For example, table 4.1 suggests that a campaign for $250 million requires about 4,964 prospects capable of committing $25,000 or more, in order to close 1,241 gifts at those levels (using a 4:1 conversion ratio). It is possible to make some assumptions about how many contacts will be needed with prospects to close a gift and about how many contacts a gift officer can reasonably be expected to complete. Simple math then determines how many gift officers need to be engaged on the campaign staff and the budget needed to support them can be calculated. Other common ratios can be used to estimate the number of support staff needed, as well as budgets for events, communications, travel, and other campaign direct expenses. In this way, the campaign budget can be built from the bottom up, based on the level of activity that the gift range chart suggests will need to be completed. The total determined through this bottom-up methodology can be compared against the top-down ratios discussed earlier to provide a check on the accuracy of the projections. In other words, if both approaches produce a budget that is approximately 10–15 percent of the campaign goal, that is probably about right.

The question of what performance metrics should be applied to the work of gift officers, in other words, how many contacts, solicitations, closed gifts, and other activities they should be expected to accomplish, is always a topic of discussion. It is explored further in chapter 6.

Development and campaign staffs are organized according to three general models. In a centralized model, all staff members report, sometimes through channels, directly to a single officer, usually a vice president. This model is typical at smaller institutions. At the other end of the spectrum, some universities have a decentralized model, in which development officers report to the heads of the units they support, that is, directors or deans, perhaps with dotted lines to the central development office. In a hybrid model, development officers generally have reporting responsibilities to both the unit head and to the central development office, which sometimes share the budget lines that support their positions and participate jointly in the evaluation of their performance.

It makes sense to organize campaign staff in a model consistent with the overall design of the campaign as well as the general administrative and budget structure of the institution. Most colleges and smaller universities build a centralized staff, while most universities with campaign goals for each academic unit have either a hybrid or decentralized structure, enabling campaign staff to work closely with deans and volunteers focused on their particular priorities.

There are potential hazards in decentralized and hybrid models. The unit-based or unit-assigned development office may feel pulled between the unit executive and the central development office. This tension can become exacerbated if there are many prospects that have more than one affiliation, for example, a couple who attended two different schools of a university. Such situations require effective systems for prospect management, including clearance and reporting. Another hazard is that a development officer working in an academic unit may be called upon to assume responsibilities not directly related to the cultivation and solicitation of donor prospects. This may include, for example, managing activities of a dean's advisory council or similar group, alumni relations activities, or communications for the college or school. Those may be important activities that someone must perform, but they need to be taken into consideration in establishing performance metrics for the individual and in projecting the number of staff needed to manage the prospect relationships that are essential to the success of the campaign.

CAMPAIGN POLICIES

This section discusses three areas of policies that need to be in place before a college or university is prepared to begin a campaign:

1. Gift acceptance policies, which generally describe what types of assets will be accepted as gifts, the procedure and authority for determining whether or not to accept a gift, and how gifted assets will be valued.
2. Donor recognition policies, which define the gifts required for the naming of campus facilities and endowment funds for various purposes. They are distinct from the gift opportunities or naming opportunities that are developed for marketing purposes during a campaign, although the latter obviously should be consistent with the former.
3. Campaign counting and reporting policies, which describe how gifts and commitments of various types will be credited toward the goal of a campaign and reflected in reports of campaign progress.

The three policy documents are interrelated and some institutions combine parts of them. The gift acceptance policy and donor recognition policy should be in place whether an institution is in a campaign or not. They are institutional policies that should be approved by the governing board. But they need to be created if they do not exist, or reviewed if they do, in anticipation of a campaign. That is essential to avoid ad hoc or rushed decisions when there is pressure to achieve dollar goals within a deadline.

Gift Acceptance Policies

The purposes of a gift acceptance policy are to ensure that the college or university does not accept gifts that may impose financial, legal, or administrative burdens, that is, to use the common phrase, "gifts that eat." Their acceptance will require the institution to spend additional funds from other sources.

Gift acceptance policies are especially important with regard to gifts of complex assets, such as real estate, closely held stock, partnership interests, art, boats, cars, and other tangible personal property. Some of the institutional risks that need to be addressed include the usefulness of the gift (for example, works of art), the liquidity of the asset (for example, closely held stock), and potential liability (a particular concern with some gifts of real estate). Most gift acceptance policies provide some flexibility and designate a gift-acceptance committee or the governing board as the ultimate authority for determining whether a specific gift meets the policies or warrants an exception.

There are several important reasons why a gift acceptance policy is essential, not only to provide legal and financial protection but also to avoid awkward situations and maintain relationships with donors. A president or a development officer who is confronted with the offer of a potentially inappropriate or risky gift, especially from an important donor or trustee, should not be in a position of having to make the decision alone. He or she should be able to point to board policy and/or refer the matter to a higher authority. The absence of a policy puts the president or the development officer under unreasonable pressure and runs the risk of making the issue personal. In such situations, clear policies and a procedure that shares decision-making authority provides protection for both the institution and the individuals involved.

Some gift acceptance policies are lengthy and include procedures for processing gifts as well as policies on acceptance. Others are brief but include references to other policies that expand on certain issues. As an example, figure 5.1 is the gift acceptance policy of Syracuse University. It is posted on the university's website, which includes links to a gift solicitation policy and a more detailed policy on the acceptance of real estate gifts. Although

The University accepts gifts in support of and to further its mission of teaching, research, and serving the public good. No gift may be counted as a contribution to the University until the asset is *irrevocably* transferred from the donor to the University and supports its mission.

Gifts-in-kind received by any office or department must be accompanied by an independent appraisal if the donor states the fair market value is more than $5,000. Gifts-in-kind that do not contribute to the University's mission will be sold.

Gifts of real estate must be approved in advance of their acceptance by the Executive Vice President/Chief Financial Officer in collaboration with the Vice President and Chief Development Officer and the University's General Counsel.

(Dated September 2005)

SOURCE: Syracuse University, (2005). "Gift Acceptance Policy." supolicies .syr.edu/ethics/gift_accept.htm (accessed June 19, 2009).

Figure 5.1.   Syracuse University: Gifts Acceptance Policy

most address common points, gift acceptance policies are unique to each institution. A search of the Web provides many additional examples.

Donor Recognition Policies

Donor recognition policies, adopted by the governing board of the institution or foundation, apply to all situations whether the institution is in a formal campaign or not, but they are especially relevant during a campaign. Most address in particular the naming of facilities, faculty positions, and academic units, such as colleges, schools, institutes, and centers.

Buildings are commonly named to recognize a gift toward construction or renovation, but colleges and universities also name existing campus facilities in recognition of a gift that goes toward some other purpose. For example, a major gift to the President's discretionary fund or to unrestricted endowment may be highly desirable, but it does not offer any inherent opportunity to recognize the donor, beyond perhaps a listing in the current annual report. In that case, naming of an existing building, lecture hall, laboratory, or some other building feature (assuming it is currently unnamed) may be a way to offer a lasting recognition of the donor's gift. But in all of these scenarios, there is a need to assure equity among donors and to ensure that the institution is not selling itself short by naming a finite inventory of campus physical assets to recognize gifts of limited impact.

As an example, the University at Albany Foundation's donor recognition policy sets specific guidelines for the naming of facilities, but also allows flexibility. It states that a gift recognized by naming of a new facility "generally" requires a gift equivalent to 15 percent of the overall cost, including "site work, equipment, and furnishings." For existing facilities, a naming gift must be equivalent to 50 percent of the renovation cost, but naming of existing facilities not under renovation is to be determined on a "case-by-case basis." The determination requires at least the approval of the university's vice president for development and "depending on the amount involved or facility or space to be named, other entities such as the University Council, SUNY System Administration or The University at Albany Foundation may need to be involved" (University at Albany, 2009).

Albany's policy takes into consideration additional features beyond cost, including "location of the space, visibility, supply/demand, and comparable facilities" (University at Albany, 2009). It is important and appropriate to take such intangibles into account. Donors of equivalent amounts should receive equivalent recognition, but the recognition conveyed by naming surely goes beyond square footage or even the cost of the facility.

An academic building or library in a central campus location is generally viewed as more prestigious and more desirable as a naming opportunity than a student residence hall located on the fringe of the campus. Naming the former thus usually requires a larger gift than naming the latter. But, of course, donors have their own perceptions, values, and motivations. An alumnus might derive emotional satisfaction from naming a residence hall where he or she once lived as a student or a building in which he or she studied, even though it might not be especially visible.

Determining the appropriate levels for recognition of gifts that establish endowed funds requires an approach similar to naming of facilities. That is, most institutions have policies that establish minimums and relate the required gift to financial cost, for example, the salary required to support a faculty position or the size or budget of an academic unit, but also allow flexibility to consider the intangible value of naming.

Endowments are usually created with the intention that they exist in perpetuity, although some donors may authorize the expenditure of principal or set a term of years after which the fund is to be terminated. Properly managed, endowment funds are indeed more lasting than buildings. The point was brought home to me one day during my tenure as vice president for development and alumni affairs at The George Washington University, as I walked around the campus with an alumnus who was considering his gift to the university's campaign. I had talked with him about endowment, but he was a real estate developer who, quite understandably, had a special appreciation for some of the new facilities that were planned or under construction and eligible to be named. It happened that at the time of this walk the university's old hospital was being demolished, since a new hospital had recently been constructed and opened across the street and the site of the old building, which had become woefully obsolete, was being cleared for redevelopment. The man asked me, "When was that old hospital built?" and I replied "in 1948." He mused, "Well, I guess the useful life of most buildings is really only about 50 or 60 years." After a pause, he said, "Tell me again about how endowed chairs work."

The endowed faculty position is one of higher education's most enduring traditions. The first endowed chair was established in 1502 at the University of Cambridge, England, by Lady Margaret Beaufort, mother of Henry VII. The Hollis Professorship of Divinity, established at Harvard in 1721, is cited as the first endowed faculty position in the United States (Luker, 2006). Naming of an endowed chair or professorship is also one of the most prestigious opportunities for philanthropy in higher education, since the position exists in perpetuity and is likely to be associated with some of the institution's most renowned professors over the years.

There are, of course, some risks for both the donor of an endowed professorship or chair as well as for the institution. There is always the possibility that some future holder of the position will be an advocate of views that were anathema to the donor, for example, a socialist may some day hold a professorship endowed by a capitalist. The two names will appear together whenever the professor is listed or presented by title. But donors also can become embarrassing to the institution and to the professor who holds a position bearing the donor's name. Indeed, this issue arose in the early 2000s with regard to endowed positions that had been named by individuals who were later involved in the corporate scandals of that period. The risk is perhaps less if the donor is deceased, but even then, history may revise its assessment, especially of political leaders. The risk can be mitigated with a clause in the gift agreement that empowers the institution to remove the donor's name under specified circumstances. Such clauses are often included in sponsorship agreements between nonprofits and celebrity athletes. But this is sensitive territory for a college or university to explore with individual donors.

There is no uniform definition of the terms "chair" or "professorship," and there are variations among institutions in the descriptions of such positions. Some institutions make distinctions among endowed faculty positions based on academic rank, discipline, and in other ways. Some permit deanships to be endowed and named and some do as well for coaching positions. Some institutions make a distinction between the endowment of a faculty position that is an existing one and one that requires a new budget line. In the latter case the required endowment may need to be sufficient to pay the full costs of the professor's salary and benefits, while an existing position may be named to recognize an endowment that supports a portion of its cost. The institution benefits, since a portion of the funds previously budgeted to support that position now may be reallocated.

Some intend that the endowment supports the professor's compensation, and some suggest that the endowment should be sufficient to also support other costs related to the professor's work, for example, research and graduate assistants. Many institutions also provide for the establishment of term professorships or chairs, that is, the donor can make a pledge to support the position with an annual gift for some period of years, during which the position is named. Once the pledge is completed, and if it is not renewed, then the position no longer carries the donor's name. Obviously, this is more practical with regard to existing faculty positions or visiting positions and would not be a good approach to creating a new budget line.

Figure 5.2 provides a sample of descriptions of endowed faculty positions from a variety of institutions. Not all of the descriptions represent formal policy statements; some are drawn from campaign websites and are more correctly called "gift opportunities." The gifts required to name faculty positions vary widely, depending on the definition of the position and also on the type of institution, especially as between independent and public institutions. Some states match private gifts made toward the endowment of professorships at public universities, which accounts for some of the differences in gifts required from private donors.

Naming gifts for academic units, especially colleges and schools within a university, are significant events. There are, after all, only so many available and creating a new one would require substantial resources. As with building naming and endowed faculty positions, determining the appropriate naming gift involves various considerations. Most would agree that a student residence hall is a less prestigious naming opportunity than the library, but the appropriate relative standard for naming a school may not be so obvious. Should the gift required to name an academic unit be based on the size of its operating budget or its enrollment? Should the gift be sufficient to endow some defined portion of the operating budget? Or should the perceived quality and prestige of the school also be considered? If the latter, by what and whose standards should that be determined?

To use the University at Albany's donor recognition policy as an example again, it ties the naming of an academic unit to its faculty size:

> The number of full-time equivalent faculty members multiplied by $250,000 dictates the amount required to permanently name a College, School, Department or Center (e.g., 50 faculty x $250,000 = $12,500,000). This gives equity to smaller units that, by virtue of their size, are not likely to be able to secure a gift of the magnitude larger units can secure. (University at Albany, 2009)

The University of Iowa and its foundation offer another example and a different approach, which bases the naming gift on three criteria: the impact of

CORNELL UNIVERSITY

Endowed professorships—to provide the long-term funding and prestige that are essential to recruiting and retaining top faculty and giving them the tools they need to succeed.

Senior Professorship—$3,000,000
Support a senior faculty member and honor the commitment of our faculty.

Assistant Professorship—$1,000,000
Help Cornell recruit junior faculty of outstanding promise.

Faculty Fellowship—$500,000
Reward superior teaching and research in all fields.

Term Professorship—$500,000
Short-term support with long-term benefits.

SOURCE: Cornell University. (2009). "Campaign Priority 2: Faculty." www.campaign.cornell.edu/faculty.cfm (accessed September 2, 2009).

IOWA STATE UNIVERSITY

Dean of a College—$3,000,000
Administrator of a Department, Program, or Institute—$2,000,000
Faculty Chair—$1,500,000
Faculty Professorship—$500,000

SOURCE: Iowa State University. (2002). *Policy for Endowed Chairs and Professorships.* www.provost.iastate.edu/faculty/awards/endowed-chairs-policy .pdf (accessed June 12, 2009).

LUTHER COLLEGE

Endowed Professorship: $600,000. An endowed professorship is usually named by the donor and held by a faculty member who has demonstrated exceptional teaching skills and has achieved distinction in his/her field. An endowed professorship exists in perpetuity.

The professorship provides funds for the annual salary of a Luther professor. The endowment also provides additional annual funds for the professor

Figure 5.2. Sample Descriptions and Gift Requirements for Endowed Chairs and Professorships

to conduct a specific research project, to attend a professional conference, or to engage in a similar activity that will enhance his/her knowledge, ability to teach, and reputation in the discipline.

SOURCE: Luther College. (2009). "Endowed Professorship: $600,000." www.luther.edu/giving/endowment/professorship/index.html (accessed June 11, 2009).

MIAMI UNIVERSITY

Chair: To establish an endowed chair, a minimum gift commitment of $1 million is required, and the chair may be restricted to specific fields of study within academic departments. The primary purpose of the endowment is to recruit faculty of stellar quality. The funds will be used to provide salary supplement to a new or existing line and also may be used to provide program support for the Chair holder. The University is responsible for the selection of chair holders.

Visiting Chair: To establish an endowed visiting chair, a minimum gift commitment of $1 million is required, depending on the size and scope of the program. The funds are to be used to supplement salary on non-tenure track faculty positions.

Professorship: To establish an endowed professorship, a minimum gift commitment of $400,000 is required. The primary purpose of the endowment is to provide support for the faculty member. The fund may be restricted by department but will be left to the dean and department chair to determine which area of study will receive the funds.

SOURCE: Miami University. (2005). "Ways to Give." www.forloveand honor.org/s/916/waystogive.aspx?sid=916&gid=1&pgid=528#section1profes sor (accessed June 11, 2009).

NORTHWESTERN UNIVERSITY

Full Professorship—$2 million
Visiting/Term Professorship—$1 million
Research Professorship—$1 million
Associate/Assistant Professorship—$1.5 million
Head Coach (depending on sport)—$1 million–$2 million

Figure 5.2. *Continued.*

SOURCE: Northwestern University. (2006). "Chairs and Professorships." development.northwestern.edu/whygive/professorships.php (accessed June 12, 2009).

SEMINOLE COMMUNITY COLLEGE FOUNDATION

An Endowed Teaching Chair is fully funded and ready to be endowed once it has reached $100,000. Since donations toward these chairs are state match eligible, a donation of $60,000 is made over a period of three years. The state match will currently provide the additional $40,000.

SOURCE: Seminole Community College Foundation. (2008). "Endowed Teaching Chairs." www.scc-fl.edu/foundation/giving/etchairs.htm (accessed June 11, 2009).

UNIVERSITY OF MICHIGAN COLLEGE OF ENGINEERING

A gift of $2 million, payable over one to five years, will name and endow a professorship. These funds will be used to underwrite partial compensatory expenses, as well as provide discretionary monies for research, travel, and other activities. Once gift payments total $1 million, the professorship is available for appointment.

SOURCE: University of Michigan College of Engineering.

VIRGINIA COMMONWEALTH UNIVERSITY

Endowed Chair—$1,000,000
Endowed Distinguished Professorship—$500,000
Endowed Professorship—$250,000

SOURCE: Virginia Commonwealth University. (2001). *University Policy: Private Support for Endowed Chairs and Professorships.* www.provost.vcu.edu/pdfs/Endchairprofpolicy32001.pdf (accessed June 12, 2009).

the gift, the unit's operating budget, and the ranking, visibility, and prestige of the unit:

> A gift recognized with the naming of a college, school, center, institute, laboratory, or major academic or program unit (hereinafter referred to as "Program") should be one that fundamentally transforms the Program. The appropriate amount and exact use of such a gift will vary among Programs, but it should always be large enough to substantially and measurably lift a Program to a new standard of excellence. . . .
>
> Specifically for college-naming, as a starting point in any discussion, it is recommended that University colleges consider only those naming gifts that will generate an annual income at least equal to one-tenth of the college's annual operating budget. (Example: A college with an annual operating budget of $50M would require a named-gift endowment of $100M assuming a 5 percent payout.) . . .
>
> A number of University colleges (particularly professional schools) are consistently ranked among the top tier of peer schools nationwide. To potentially permanently attach a donor's name to a nationally ranked program, with its increased visibility and prestige, might reasonably be expected to require a more sizeable contribution threshold than would a college with less potential for national prominence. (University of Iowa, 2008)

Scholarship endowments are more scalable than chairs or professorships or academic units. That is, the scholarship is generally limited to the endowment income and even a modest award may have a significant impact for a particular student. But there is a cost to managing small endowment funds as well as matching the recipients of scholarship awards with the specific endowed funds that support them. Most colleges and universities establish a minimum amount that is acceptable to create a separate, named endowment fund of any type. In the case of scholarships, that minimum may be acceptable, while more is better.

Unrestricted endowment is greatly desired, since the income from such funds offers the most flexibility to the institution's leaders. Historically, a high portion of unrestricted endowment gifts has come from bequests, in which the donor has named the institution's endowment but no specific use for the income. Others may prefer to restrict the gift at least to a specific program or unit of interest to them.

Unrestricted endowment is an objective in many campaigns and institutions creatively package unrestricted endowment gifts as naming opportunities at various levels, defining for example, president's funds, dean's funds, and chair's funds. The donor is recognized through the naming of the endowment; the income may be used at the discretion of the president or another officer as provided. For example, Mount Holyoke College's campaign endowment gift opportunities ("Accomplish Great Things: The Campaign for Mount Holyoke") include a Presidential Innovation Fund for New Initiatives at $4 million, a Dean of Faculty's Discretionary Fund at $1 million, and Library Acquisition Funds and Departmental Funds at $100,000 (Mount Holyoke College, 2009). To make the distinction again, these are gift opportunities designed to capture the interest of campaign donors and to give them some standard for their gifts. Unrestricted endowments are generally not encompassed within a formal donor recognition policy, except to the extent that there is a minimum for creating any endowment fund.

Establishing donor recognition opportunities is an area that requires judgment. Gift opportunities may be determined both with reference to cost of whatever purpose is endowed (construction or renovation cost for a facility, the salary of a professor, the operating budget of an academic unit) and intangibles (the prestige or promise of a school, the visibility and use of a building), but there also needs to be a consideration of the market. That is, establishing the required gift levels also requires considering how previous donors have been recognized at the particular college or university, what other institutions have received for similar purposes, and the interests and capacity of the particular institution's known constituency. As discussed in chapter 4 with regard to creating the gift range chart, it would be foolish not to have a $5 million naming opportunity on the list if there is a known prospect with that capacity. But what if the target of the prospect's interest really requires a $10 million gift, which the donor really cannot afford to make? Is $5 million better than zero, especially if $5 million can still have impact and there are no $10 million prospects in sight? Such questions defy easy answers in real life.

Donor recognition policies need to provide the flexibility for the governing board, or perhaps a gift acceptance or campaign steering committee, to make decisions in the best interests of the institution. But flexibility complicates things and raises risks. For example, perhaps it is believed that naming a laboratory for a deceased alumnus in exchange for a relatively modest gift now will establish a relationship with his or her family that will lead to more gifts in the future. The naming may provide unique opportunities for stewardship and the full value of the naming may need to be considered over the entire course of those relationships, not just at the time of naming. But how will that recognition be justified in the case of others who may die and whose assets may offer less potential?

Scenarios similar to that just described do occur and some flexibility is required. But they raise the issue of equity and fairness among donors and the recognition given for gifts that represent equivalent sacrifice. They present the risk of hurt feelings and damaged relationships. But there is an additional risk as well. If recognition becomes entirely subjective and negotiable, that erodes the culture of philanthropy over time. It turns fundraising into sales and converts a gift into a purchase, at a negotiable price.

It is only realistic to acknowledge that exceptions may need to be made in order to maintain and expand relationships between people and their institutions. But they need to be carefully considered in the best long-term interests of the college or university and the procedure for considering them should include more than the president's or chief development officer's judgment call.

Campaign Counting and Reporting Policies

In the historical capital campaign, what counted toward the goal of the campaign was rather straightforward—cash and formal pledges that would be paid on a timetable consistent with the need to pay the contractors who were constructing the building for which the campaign was undertaken. But as the comprehensive campaign emerged as the standard model in higher education since the 1970s, encompassing gifts for endowment as well as capital projects and planned as well as outright gifts, differences in how campaigns counted certain types of commitments became problematic. They made it difficult for institutional leaders to benchmark against others in setting their goals or to evaluate their own performance. It also became complicated to determine exactly how to recognize donors whose responses to the campaign might include complex financial arrangements. The question of how certain commitments would be counted became interrelated with the decision about what the goal could be, so counting decisions needed to be made as a matter of policy during the campaign's planning phase. There was for a long time little guidance available.

Responding to the need for clarity, in 1979 the Council for Advancement and Support developed recommendations on how campaign commitments should be counted and reported. Those guidelines have been revised several times since, most recently in 2008. Perhaps the most complex area involves the counting and reporting of revocable deferred gifts (e.g., bequest expectancies), irrevocable planned gifts (e.g., charitable remainder trusts and charitable gift annuities), and conditional pledges. The 2008 revision of the CASE guidelines addresses these areas in particular and establishes some recommended best practices, while also permitting flexibility for institutions to adopt policies that address their particular strategic directions and purposes in undertaking the campaign.

The campaign guidelines are one component of the larger *CASE Reporting Standards and Management Guidelines,* fourth edition (CASE, 2009a). This document establishes the requirements for reporting to CASE's annual campaign survey as well as the Voluntary Support of Education survey conducted by the Council for Aid to Education and offers recommended guidelines related to the management of fundraising programs and campaigns. They are detailed and a full discussion is beyond the scope of this book. The full document is available from the CASE website (www.case.org; CASE, 2009b), and it is an indispensable resource for campaign planning.

Following the guidelines provides the president, the chief advancement officer, and the board with a sound basis for explaining campaign policies and communicating the complex nature of a comprehensive campaign to all of their constituencies.

While the campaign guidelines allow for institutional discretion on a number of points, CASE provides five fundamental principles with regard to campaign counting and reporting. All serve the purpose of honesty, transparency, and clarity in communicating campaigns to both internal and external constituents:

1. Count only those gifts and pledges actually received or committed during the specific period of time identified for the campaign in campaign totals.
2. The advance-gifts phase of a campaign is always a part of the designated campaign period. Report commitments (including pledges) for this phase that the institution receives during this specified period within the larger campaign period.
3. Count each gift or pledge to only one campaign. In other words, a pledge made, but not fulfilled, during one campaign should not have the balance counted in a new campaign. The original pledge was made for one, and only one, campaign. Do not count payments received on pledges made prior to the current campaign, including those made between campaigns.
4. The value of any canceled pledges should be subtracted from campaign totals when it is determined they will not be realized. Institutions should follow an annual pledge review or write-off process that they continue in a multiyear campaign.
5. To ensure clarity, transparency, and accountability, decisions about what types of gifts will be accepted, counted, and reported during the campaign should be made prior to the start of the campaign, announced to appropriate audiences at the outset of the campaign, and remain consistent throughout the full course of the campaign (CASE, 2009a, pp. 86–87).

REFERENCES

Council for Advancement and Support of Education (CASE). (1990). *Expenditures in Fund Raising, Alumni Relations, and Other Constituent (Public) Relations.* Washington, DC: Author.

———. (2009a). *CASE Reporting Standards and Management Guidelines for Educational Fundraising.* 4th edition. Washington, DC: Author.

———. (2009b). "Home Page." www.case.org (accessed May 26, 2009).

Dove, Kent. (2000). *Conducting a Successful Capital Campaign.* 2nd edition. San Francisco: Jossey-Bass.

Gearhart, G. David. (2006). *Philanthropy, Fundraising, and the Capital Campaign: A Practical Guide.* Washington, DC: National Association of College and University Business Officers.

Kihlstedt, Andrea. (2005). *Capital Campaigns: Strategies that Work.* 2nd edition. Sudbury, MA: Jones and Bartlett.

Luker, Ralph E. (2006). "Sit in My Chair." *Inside Higher Ed,* December 4. www.insidehighered.com/views/2006/12/04/luker (accessed June 11, 2009).

Mount Holyoke College. (2009). "Endowment Naming Opportunities." www.mtholyoke.edu/offices/develop/campaign2010/endowgiftopps.php (accessed May 21, 2009).

University at Albany. (2009). "Recognition Opportunities." www.albany.edu/uafoundation/policies_and_procedures_124.htm (accessed May 21, 2009).

University of Iowa. (2008). *Named Gift Recognition Guidelines of the University of Iowa and the University of Iowa Foundation.* June. www.uiowa.edu/president/naming_guidelines/naming_guidelines_0608.pdf (accessed May 21, 2009).

6

Executing the Campaign

The campaign begins with the quiet phase (also often called the silent phase, nucleus phase, or advance phase), in which the top prospects and key insiders are solicited. As the quiet phase proceeds, the campaign leadership evaluates results and adjusts the campaign's working goal, priorities, and objectives as necessary to reflect ongoing experience. Once the advance gift prospects have been solicited and their decisions are known, the campaign is ready to be formally announced at the kickoff. Hopefully, the goal announced will be what was established as the working goal or even higher, depending on results of the solicitations during the quiet phase. The campaign then enters the public phase, but that is not to say that it has become a broad-based effort. The annual fund is the vehicle for soliciting all of the institution's constituents during the public phase, but the focus of campaign activity remains on major gifts throughout its duration.

The president's activities during the public phase of the campaign include providing energy and vision to the campaign, providing the public face of the institution and the campaign at a multitude of events, participating in the cultivation and solicitation of major gift prospects, and monitoring the campaign's progress. Again, although the annual fund is included and, at research universities, noncontractual grants for research and programs are generally counted as well, most of the effort in the campaign is devoted to the cultivation and solicitation of prospects for major and planned gifts.

This chapter begins with a discussion of the major gifts fundraising process, with an emphasis on the president's role. It then discusses some broad strategies for solicitation and concludes with some metrics of performance. While this chapter discusses the *process* of major gifts fundraising, it does not delve into specific techniques for cultivating prospects and soliciting gifts. Chapter 7, titled "The Art of Fundraising," considers cultivation and solicitation in more detail.

THE MAJOR GIFT PROCESS

Figure 6.1 provides a visual illustration of the major gifts fundraising process. The vocabulary of major gifts fundraising—the terms "prospects," "cultivation," "solicitation," and so forth—is well known and the visual in figure 6.1 may seem at first to be fairly simple. But there is more than meets the eye, and each step can be unbundled to gain a deeper understanding of fundraising and of people.

Figure 6.1 is my creation, and I have adapted some of the concepts according to my own experience and thinking, but the ideas and the terminology are based primarily on the pioneering thinking of three leaders in the educational fundraising field: David Dunlop, G. T. "Buck" Smith, and Henry Rosso. Both Dunlop and Smith graduated from Cornell and began their higher education careers there. Dunlop remained with Cornell throughout his career and eventually retired to become one of the best-known authors and speakers on major gifts fundraising. Smith left Cornell to return to his undergraduate alma mater, the College of Wooster, and served as vice president for development there for many years, eventually moving to the presidency at Chapman University. He is now president of Davis & Elkins College in West Virginia. Rosso was a fundraising consultant who was instrumental in founding the Fund Raising School, now a part of the Center on Philanthropy at Indiana University, and served as the center's first director. His book, *Achieving Excellence in Fund Raising*, the second edition of which was edited by Eugene Tempel in 2003 following Rosso's death, remains one of the best-known volumes in the field. Together, these three thoughtful practitioners defined the essential con-

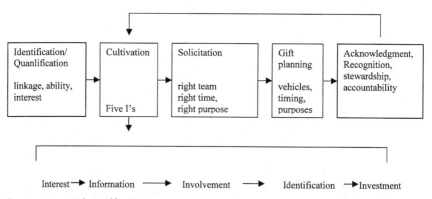

Figure 6.1. Major Gifts Process. *Sources*: Based on Smith (1977), Dunlop (2002), and Rosso (2003).

cepts that still underlie major gifts fundraising and introduced the basic vocabulary of the field.

The Cultivation Cycle

Figure 6.1 portrays the major gifts process from two perspectives. The top portion depicts the process from the perspective of the fundraiser. In the first step, a donor prospect is *identified and qualified*. The relationship between the individual and the institution is then systematically *cultivated*, through a series of planned and systematic initiatives or "moves" (Dunlop, 2002). When the relationship has proceeded to the point that the individual is prepared to give, the *solicitation* occurs, but that is not the end of the process, even if the response is favorable.

In many cases, the prospect's response to a solicitation is not an unambiguous "yes," but rather the expression of a desire to make a gift accompanied by some concerns about the feasibility of the proposed amount and/or the structuring of the gift and/or the specific purposes toward which the gift should be applied. There is often a need for *gift planning*, a term I use to mean more than planned giving as that phrase is generally understood. The gift may indeed involve some form of planned giving, perhaps combined with an outright gift, but there may also be a need for discussion of the purposes of the gift, including development of a memorandum of understanding or gift agreement, the structuring of payments, and other details. What I am calling "gift planning" encompasses all of these considerations and might be thought of as negotiating the gift, although the latter term has a commercial connotation that I generally prefer to avoid.

Once the gift has been completed, the process continues with *acknowledgment* of the gift, *recognition* of the donor, and *stewardship* of the ongoing relationship with the donor. Stewardship includes accountability for sound management of the gift to assure that it meets the intended purposes and has an impact that demonstrates its value. This post-gift activity and responsibility then merges into continuing cultivation that may lead to additional gifts in the future. Of course, these latter stages of the process may not be completed within the span of a single campaign and are ongoing activities that will continue beyond its conclusion. They are indeed part of preparation for the next campaign. A fuller discussion of these activities is deferred to chapter 8, where they are explored in the context of post-campaign activity.

A common concern is how long the process requires. That is, how long does it take to move a newly identified prospect from identification to the point of readiness for a major gift? A common answer is about eighteen to thirty-six months, although there is obviously a wide variation, depending on the history of the individual's relationship with the institution. There are some prospects, including some entrepreneurial donors, who may be ready to jump in to support a new and exciting idea with very little cultivation.

Others may require years of cultivation and the gift may not mature for a long time. Another question that is asked is how many contacts or visits are required to move a prospect across the continuum to readiness. Again, there is no pat answer, although some say that it requires an average of about seven. I am not aware of any source for that number nor any research to support it—it may just be a part of fundraising legend.

The Five I's

The bottom portion of figure 6.1 depicts an individual's emerging relationship with an institution. The "Five I's" are generally attributed to G. T. Smith (1977), but others have offered variations. It is important to acknowledge that although the Five I's is a model held at least implicitly by most major gift practitioners, it has been challenged by some scholars. For example, Kathleen Kelly in her 1998 book *Effective Fund Raising Management*, states that the model is inconsistent with communications theory and notes that "donors are not passive participants who can be programmed to give; nor are they a predictable homogeneous group." She writes that the "effects [of fundraising activities] do form a hierarchy, with awareness as the lowest effect and behavior as one of the highest. The effects represent impacts of fundraising efforts; they do not, however, represent a progression whereby an individual moves from a cognitive, to an attitudinal, to a behavioral state" (Kelly, 1998, p. 356).

However, whatever its theoretical weaknesses, the Five I's model is well established in the fundraising practitioner literature, and its assumptions play out in the moves or initiatives undertaken with campaign prospects. According to this model, an individual's relationship with an institution begins with some level of *interest* (one of the three criteria for identifying a prospect). Interest is enhanced through the provision of additional *information*. A key stage in the process is the individual's *involvement* with the institution, with substantive involvement having the strongest effect in leading to the next I—*identification*.

This is a different use of the term "identification" than in the top portion of the diagram; it means that the individual comes to psychologically identify with the institution, to consider it as his or her own and to incorporate an association with it as part of his or her personal identity. We see this identification manifested all the time by window stickers on cars, sweatshirts, and other items bearing college and university names and logos. Identification with an institution of higher education is often revealed early in conversations with people. According to the Five I's model, only when the individual has come to identify with the institution is he or she prepared for *investment*, that is, the giving of a major gift.

The cultivation phase of the major gifts fundraising process usually involves systematic efforts to move prospects along this continuum to the point of readiness to invest, thus a fundraiser's activities consistent of a series of planned moves to encourage this progression. The term "moves" was introduced by Dunlop (2002). He now prefers to speak of "initiatives," thinking that "moves" may sound manipulative, but the latter is a well-established term in the fundraising field, and major gift officers continue to describe their work in terms of managing their moves.

It is important to emphasize that relationships with major gift prospects are *managed.* That is, initiatives are undertaken according to a planned strategy and timetable, not randomly or just opportunistically. The individuals who maintain the relationship are, in Dunlop's terms, primes or secondaries. That is, more than one individual on the campus may have a relationship with a given prospect, although there needs to be a clear understanding of relative roles. In most prospect management systems, secondaries are required to clear contacts with the prospect through the primary, and all contacts are to be reported to a central database.

It is also important to distinguish the role of the person or persons who holds the relationship with the prospect from that of the prospect manager or relationship manager. Prospect relationships are assigned to a prospect manager, usually a development officer, who is responsible for tracking and initiating moves regarding that relationship. The development officer who is managing the relationship does not necessarily have an exclusive or even the strongest relationship with the prospect. It may be the president, a dean, a faculty member, a volunteer, or someone else who has the relationship with the prospect. In such a situation, the prospect manager's role is to assure that the president or other principal is prompted to undertake initiatives, that initiatives are followed up, and that the relationship develops as planned—to assure that moves are made, but not necessarily to make them. This is something like the role of a sales manager, who may or may not also be a salesperson.

There are, of course, many cases in which a development officer does indeed have the closest relationship with a prospect and functions as both the relationship manager and as principal in the relationship. In terms of the football analogy described in chapter 3, the development officer may be both the quarterback and runner. This has become more common in recent decades as professional staff have taken on larger roles in cultivation and solicitation. But it is important to maintain the distinctions

There are likely to be prospects for whom the president is the prime, but it is usually essential for the president to be supported by a professional who is managing those relationships. That may be a vice president or a major or principal gifts officer who is in close contact and communication with the president on a regular basis and who tracks and prompts activity as needed. Most presidents' schedules are hectic, and they are frequently distracted by other demands. It would be easy to postpone or neglect a call, visit, or other activity with a prospect unless the president is supported by someone who is focused on key relationships and is monitoring their status every day. Presidents may sometimes find prompting by a development officer to be mildly annoying, but most know, at least in their hearts, that it is necessary.

Where a development officer plays both roles, there is still a need to engage others in the relationship, including the president, deans, volunteer leaders, and other key people, as appropriate. Multiple actors in the process are essential to develop the relationship and maintain it over the long term despite possible transitions in the staff and institutional leadership. As discussed in chapter 3, successful fundraising is almost always a team effort.

Identifying and Qualifying Prospects

Chapter 4 included some discussion of techniques for identifying potential prospects. But a name on a list does not a prospect make. Further insight is needed to determine the likelihood that the individual will make a gift to the campaign.

Henry Rosso is credited with defining the criteria for qualifying a major gift prospect: linkage, ability, and interest (Seiler, 2003, p. 28). For higher education institutions, generally all three criteria must be met or it is unlikely that the individual should be considered a bona fide prospect.

Not every living person is a prospect for a given institution, even if they are known to be wealthy and philanthropic. Most major individual donors to colleges and universities have some linkage; they may be alumni, parents, grateful patients of a university medical center, or leaders in the community where the institution is located. They are not usually strangers or names culled from a national or even a local list of wealthy people. The latter are what I call "fantasy prospects." It is just not a realistic list for most institutions.

Foundations and corporations may respond to the power of a proposal, but individuals generally provide major gifts to institutions with which they have some natural connection. Of course, most, though not all, people who have the capacity to make a major gift will have some linkage with some institution of higher education. If they are not themselves college graduates, they likely will have an established connection with some college or university through their family, geographic proximity, or in some other way. Some people have such linkages with multiple institutions, but some relationships predominate. They are usually obvious or readily discovered.

For that reason, direct competition among colleges and universities for the attention of individual prospects is not the norm. Surely, there are instances in which an individual has linkages with multiple institutions; perhaps a spouse or other family members have attended other colleges or universities, or a local business leader maintains relationships with two colleges located nearby. But, in general, linkages with one institution are stronger than with others and prospects sort themselves out naturally among them. That means that it is also generally not time well spent in attempting to cultivate a prospect who is known to have a strong relationship with another institution.

The ability to give is, of course, one of the essential criteria for a major gift prospect. As the old expression goes, you can't get blood from a stone, and it is axiomatic that people who make major gifts are those with the resources to do so. But, consistent with Benjamin Franklin's fundraising advice mentioned in chapter 1, "about some you may be mistaken." In other words, ability sometimes exists where it is not obvious.

One of the largest donors to The George Washington University during my years as vice president for development and alumni affairs was a retired member of the faculty. He was stereotypically professorial in his appearance and demeanor, quiet, low-key, thoughtful. I never would have thought him to be wealthy and, indeed, he self-identified by coming to visit me at my office one day early in my tenure. We engaged in a pleasant conversation about education and academic life and at the conclusion of the meeting he handed me a check, saying that he would like to support a graduate student award. It was more than a token, but not an overwhelming sum. That began a series of annual conversations, all at his initiative, after which he would hand me a check (or a security endorsed to the university) in what became increasing amounts. My initiatives to communicate with him were generally unrewarded; he would pick the time and place for any interaction. He would seem mildly displeased if I called him, and he would never respond to any other communication until it was time for his annual visit to my office. The prospect researchers could uncover little about him except for scholarly publications he had produced when an active member of the faculty and basic directory information.

After several years of his regular visits, on one occasion the scope of the conversation expanded. How, he was wondering, could the quality of an academic department be most quickly advanced—by recruiting the best graduate students, whom great professors would be attracted to teach, or by recruiting the best professors, who would attract brilliant students to study? In other words, he asked me, if the goal were to strengthen one of our departments, would philanthropy be most effective if directed toward graduate student fellowships or endowed professorships? We discussed the matter for a long time, and he decided that an endowed professorship would be the best approach. Concluding the meeting, he said, "Well, I would like to create one of those. How could I do that?" I was, of course, happy to provide instruction.

Over the next few years, his philanthropy expanded, he endowed *several* professorships, and one of our academic departments was significantly enhanced as a result. And he gradually opened up with me and provided more of his story. He had married the only child of a wealthy family, whose parents had passed away, leaving him to manage the family's resources, which he had done successfully. He had remained true to his values as an academic and never engaged in conspicuous consumption. His own children had succeeded on their own, and he felt no need to provide additionally for them. The center of his professional life had been as a member of our faculty for forty years, during which he always lamented the inadequate resources available to his department. He and his wife were now in their eighties, and he was preparing to direct his assets in a way that could bring maximum benefit for others who would follow in his path in future years. At a time when strategic philanthropy was still a relatively new idea, he carefully and methodically invested in his old department with a clear objective.

This donor is one case among many that suggest it is a mistake to overlook those who have strong linkage to the college or university but whose wealth may not be obvious or even determinable through the usual tools of prospect research. Indeed, among Rosso's (2003) three criteria, linkage may be the most important as a starting point. Some people of only modest wealth may become, if family and other life circumstances permit and if they are assisted by skilled gift planners, major donors to the institutions with which they have strong bonds.

The third of Rosso's criteria is interest. An individual may have linkage and the ability to give, but absent interest, it is not going to happen. As the old saying goes, "if I had a dollar" for every time I was disappointed by the lack of interest in an otherwise promising prospect, I would be a wealthy man. As director and later a vice president for development, on too many occasions I visited a prospect who had known wealth and whose linkages with the institution were strong—perhaps as an alumnus, a parent, or in some other way—but who simply had no interest in providing support. Perhaps some of that experience was related to gaps in the institution's alumni relations and development efforts in previous decades, but some of it is just human reality. Some people are just not philanthropic. Others support institutions in their own communities and more highly value the visibility, recognition, and social position that come from directing their philanthropy locally rather than to the college or university far away that they attended years ago. And, for various reasons, some just do not see higher education as an important cause and prefer to allocate their giving to nonprofit organizations that serve other important purposes to which they are also linked and in which they simply have greater interest, perhaps based on philosophy, voluntary service, or some aspect of family or life experience.

As an example, there was an alumnus of The George Washington University whom I first visited in the mid-1980s, in the midst of the first of two campaigns that I directed during my tenure as vice president there. He was a graduate of the university's law school and was at the time of that first visit an executive in a corporation. On that occasion, he explained to me that he knew very little about the university in general, never having ventured far beyond the law school during his years on campus. Moreover, his current work was that of a corporate executive rather than a practicing attorney, so he also did not have much interest in the law school specifically. He explained that his education had provided a good background for his career, but he was not especially interested in supporting the law school or any other aspect of the university. He was, indeed, on the board of other institutions closer to his home and with which he and his family also had relationships. And his wife had attended another university, in which she had some interest.

I am sure that my contact report from this visit noted the facts and suggested that he be considered only as a prospect for annual giving, not a major gift. He did make annual gifts in subsequent years, for which I provided a friendly acknowledgment, but I did not return to visit him.

Over the next decade, his situation changed dramatically. To preserve his anonymity, I will just say that he became involved in the technology boom of the 1990s, left the firm at which I had first visited him, and amassed a considerable fortune. I went to see him again in the context of the university's next campaign, returned again together with the president, and yet again to follow up on the subject of his gift to the campaign.

I asked about his philanthropy, and he proceeded to describe plans that he and his wife were formulating for the creation of their own nonprofit organization. Again, to preserve his anonymity, I will just say that it would offer programs related to children, although its focus was indeed somewhat more specific than that. He explained that he respected the work of the university and that he would continue to support it modestly, but that he and his wife wanted to create something new that would not have the constraints of affiliation with a larger institution. They had their own well-developed philosophy about how such programs should be operated and preferred to have the freedom to implement a new approach within their control. I tried to steer the conversation toward the law school, but he reminded me that he had never practiced law. I discussed the business school and its programs related to entrepreneurship, among others, but he displayed no interest. He listened when I discussed the university's priorities, but his face lit up with excitement when he described his own plans. They would be the focus of his most substantial philanthropy. I could tell that a train was rolling down the track at high speed and concluded that I couldn't stop it. The best I might do would be to catch a ride.

In following months, the president and I saw him again and we delivered a series of proposals. We suggested how one of the university's programs could be the research arm of his new organization. He was not too interested. We followed up with proposals for endowed professorships and support for other related university programs and explained how the university would work as a partner in his new endeavor. Some of the proposals were quite creative and, I believed, compelling. He did make a major gift to the university in response to one component of our proposals, but the largest portion of his philanthropy continued to be focused on the development of the new organization that he and his wife would found. In the end, he had linkage and ability, but his interest was not with our institution or its programs, and there was little that we could do to alter that, at least not within the window of my opportunity with him.

Sometimes those who have linkage and ability but no interest should be appropriately coded, and the fundraiser should just move on. Creativity and persistence are important qualities in successful fundraising, but there also needs to be a judgment about the time and cost invested in pursuit of a prospect who has made his or her alternative interest clear. And, of course, continued pursuit of a prospect who has convincingly expressed a lack of interest may be inappropriate and counterproductive, but the relationship with a prospect who has high capacity and linkage should never be totally abandoned, even when it seems to have run its course with a less than pleasing outcome. When there is linkage and ability, other things may change—lives evolve, interests shift, opportunities arise, and skillful cultivation can sometimes develop or resuscitate a relationship despite initial—or even prolonged—discouragement. My own experience includes prospects whose lack of interest at one time in their relationship with the institution was reversed at a later point in their lives or careers or with some intervening event, for example, the enrollment of a son or daughter, retirement, or something else that changed their perspective. "No interest, period," is difficult to overcome. But a highly tuned ear may hear some latent interest—at least some glimmer—in even the most reluctant prospect. It may be enhanced if consistently and respectfully developed over time. It may mature, later in this campaign or in the next one.

One of the benefits of a campaign is that it creates intensity. The cultivation cycle is pursued on a time frame that is hoped to produce a gift commitment within the period of the campaign. It brings discipline and accountability to those undertaking the fundraising and, for some prospects, creates a structure within which it is logical to consider a gift. But that also can present a problem, for reasons related to the preceding discussion. There is also the risk that the pressure of the campaign deadline will be a reason to abandon unpromising situations prematurely, especially those that may take years or decades to mature. Prospects may be lost in the cracks for a long time, after which their interests and support may have drifted elsewhere.

David Dunlop introduced the concept of nurturing fundraising, a long-term process in which maintaining the relationship takes priority over solicitation. In this approach, relationships may be cultivated for decades, even a lifetime. The gift is solicited when the prospect is ready and occurs naturally as a culmination of the relationship, often without prodding. It is a process that rises above and continues across any single campaign. Of course, as Dunlop notes, it is an approach that can be applied to only a few prospects, those with the most potential to make a principal or transformational ultimate gift (Dunlop, 2002). In the heat of a campaign, and with inevitable turnover in presidents, deans, trustees, development officers, and other campus leaders, it is important than some key prospects continue to be followed systematically over the longer term, even though their philanthropy may not benefit the current campaign. The incentives that the campaign presents for resolution works against this approach, but it is a part of a president's responsibility to the institution to assure that systems are in place to support the continuing long-term cultivation of institutional relationships with at least a small number of individuals.

Cultivating Donor Relationships

Cultivation is the second step on the top portion of figure 6.1, and it expands into the Five I's. The work of cultivation is to move qualified prospects across the continuum from interest, however mild or latent it may be, toward investment. As described earlier, this is accomplished through a series of initiatives that are planned and executed according to a strategy for each prospect. They may include what Dunlop calls background moves and foreground moves. A background move involves an opportunity for engagement that is not created with regard to the individual prospect; it would include, for example, inviting the individual to an event or a game that is otherwise taking place and which provides an opportunity to build the relationship with that individual. A foreground move is more specific; it is planned just for that individual. It might include a visit by the president or a development officer, a dinner planned to recognize the individual, granting of an award to the individual, or some other activity that is designed with the entire purpose of advancing the relationship with that prospect; in other words, it is planned just for him or her and would not otherwise occur (Dunlop, 2002).

Some people, probably including some college and university presidents and, I must say, even some development officers, are uncomfortable about the idea of cultivating relationships in such a deliberate way. It may seem too commercial, like sales, or not consistent with the culture and values of higher education. Some may feel it to be manipulative, perhaps even dishonest—intentionally creating a relationship for the purpose of a predetermined outcome. Some may just find it difficult to have the patience for what may be a long and slow process.

But, it is not different from courtship. Dates for dinner and the movies and sending flowers (if anybody does that anymore) are often actions in pursuit of a desired outcome as well, whether just a closer relationship or marriage. As in fundraising, both parties are willing participants in the process and the result is often mutually rewarding. There are few who would be misled or displeased about the motivations behind such initiatives, in either aspect of life. And patience is often required.

Discomfort with the cultivation of prospects may reflect the feeling that making a major gift to a college or university is somehow a bad thing that an individual will come to regret, that securing a gift is somehow extracting resources and imposing hardship on the donor. But that perception is not supported by any experience. First, again, people generally understand where it is going when a development officer or the president comes to visit; they are willing participants in the cultivation process. Gifts are voluntary, and most people with the capacity to make them are too experienced and sophisticated to respond to pressure. I have never known or heard of a donor who was unhappy about having made a major gift—leaving aside, of course, some instances in which a donor may not be happy about how the gift has been managed or used. For most if not all, seeing the results of their philanthropy is a rewarding and pleasurable experience. Chapter 7 will return to some of these points.

Moving from left to right across the cultivation continuum, the prospect's interest may be enhanced by providing more information, the second of the Five I's. More information does not, of course, automatically lead to commitment, but it is necessary to provide a foundation for the individual's greater involvement. Some might call this portion of the process donor education, although others may find that term patronizing. It is a process of informing a prospect about the institution and its programs as well as about its directions and goals. But information alone is not motivating and the individual's relationship with the institution needs to progress to the next stages—involvement and identification—before a prospect is ready for a major gift.

The most critical step in the process is *involvement*. At first, involvement may be in the form of Dunlop's background moves—perhaps the individual attends some social or athletic events, speaks to a class, or engages in some other way with the institution's programs and personalities. But, substantive involvement, in which the individual begins to accept some responsibility for the institution itself, is an inflection point that can lead ultimately to the next I—identification. To use the courtship analogy again, substantive involvement is like becoming engaged (or going steady, if anyone does that anymore); it involves commitment and obligation.

There are many ways in which individuals can become involved with a college or university in a substantive way and institutions can create such opportunities. For example, institutional planning in advance of the campaign can engage various task forces and advisory groups that increase both individuals' knowledge and involvement with the institution. A campaign planning study or feasibility study, perhaps involving individual interviews as well as focus groups, both informs prospective donors about the institution and involves them in the process by seeking their perceptions and opinions.

But involvement can be more subtle as well. When I served as director of development at the University of Maryland–College Park, I was—almost accidentally—charged with directing a modest campaign to raise endowment for a research center, which had received a challenge grant that needed to be matched. Frankly, the challenge grant had been unanticipated. In those days (but surely not now) it was possible for a research center director to apply for and receive a grant without the knowledge of the senior administration. So, this challenge just arrived, and there was little time to prepare for a campaign following the usual model.

Our first thought was to enlist a campaign chair and assemble a leadership committee, but our efforts to do so proved challenging. The director of the center and I, with participation by the president and others as needed, pursued an alternative strategy. The president would ask that individuals meet with us to provide us with guidance and advice on our project. We then would send a draft of our case statement and ask that they carefully review it, mark it up, and prepare for a meeting with us to discuss their thoughts about it. We emphasized that we were not coming to solicit a gift on that occasion. We conducted the meetings as if they were feasibility study interviews, asking for reactions to our plan and our draft case and the individuals' judgment about how others might respond, what changes we might make to our case to make it more appealing, and frankly acknowledging the challenges we were facing. We did not, in fact, usually solicit a gift, but in many of these meetings the individual turned the conversation in that direction and requested a proposal or some other follow-up. Working in this way, revising our draft for each meeting, we indeed raised about half of the required funds. A single donor then was impressed with our success and committed the other half to successfully complete the effort.

It was an unusual way to proceed, driven by the circumstances, but on reflection I learned something from it. It illustrated the sometimes subtle but important difference between providing information and gaining involvement. The individuals with whom we met were never formally involved—there was never a campaign chair or committee. But our approach—asking for guidance and advice on the case—had involved them in a way that did stimulate their thinking about our program. Had the case statement ever been finalized as a glossy printed brochure, it would have provided information. But as a draft on which comments were sought, it was a vehicle for involvement, however modest. The case statement remained a draft through dozens of versions and was never finalized.

Of course, ongoing involvement is desirable to build the individual's psychological identity with the institution. Formal advisory boards and councils, often related to specific schools, centers, or programs, are one approach that offers additional opportunities.

Advisory boards and councils in higher education have proliferated in the past decade. Although there are no historical data to track their growth, advisory councils have gained wider attention in recent years, leading to the study conducted in 2007 by the Association of Governing Boards (AGB), which was referenced earlier in this book (Worth, 2008). That study identified hundreds of such boards at both independent and public universities, likely just scratching the surface.

Advisory councils provide an intermediate step in involvement. Individuals who join such a council accept some responsibility for the institution, but it is a step short of election to the governing or foundation board. It can be an opportunity for the individual to become more familiar with the institution and its people and provide useful service without the legal responsibilities of trusteeship. For the institution, the council can be a testing ground, a kind of farm club, through which it can identify those with the interest, talent, and capabilities that might qualify them for higher office as a member of the governing or foundation board or as a campaign volunteer.

To be effective in attracting and engaging strong members, advisory councils need to be carefully defined and managed. Few affluent or influential people will be attracted to join a council with the sole purpose of raising funds. At the same time, institutions create lay advisory councils at least in part as a vehicle for involving potential donors and fundraising volunteers; otherwise, advice might be obtained as needed on an individual basis or from specialists who are not donor prospects.

Typical advisory council job descriptions, which were examined in AGB's 2007 study, include a balanced array of responsibilities, encompassing giving and fundraising but also other purposes. For example, the following responsibilities are often listed:

- Serve as the institution's advocates and ambassadors, increasing the institution's visibility and image within council members' own communities, professions, and industries
- Provide strategic advice to the president, dean, or program director (Some councils do advise on academic and curricular matters, especially in professional schools such as business, law, and engineering. But other job descriptions clarify that the council provides advice on strategic issues, not curriculum.)
- Provide nonfinancial resources, for example, guest lecturers for classes, consulting opportunities for faculty, contacts and relationships with potential employers of students, and so forth

- Participate in campus events
- Give and assist in fundraising (Some descriptions are more subtle, saying something like "help identify opportunities for financial support.")

Including giving and fundraising as one of the responsibilities of an advisory council is essential to make expectations in that regard explicit. But defining broader responsibilities of the council helps to make membership more attractive and, in addition, to engage its members in a substantive way that may lead to identification and investment.

Some may think that the broader responsibilities of advisory councils are just window dressing and that the real purpose in creating them is the cultivation of potential donors and fundraising volunteers. But, indeed, AGB's study found that both presidents and deans valued their councils for their non-monetary contributions as well. Most presidents and deans said that the top benefit gained from the council was relationships with external constituencies *other than donors*, including, for example, industry and government. Presidents saw their councils as vehicles for getting to know potential governing board candidates and as a way to involve individuals who might prefer to not carry the formal responsibilities of trusteeship. A significant number of deans pointed to the assistance of the advisory council in securing jobs and internships for students, and a few noted that a strong external advisory council may be a source of political leverage within the institution itself. But, unsurprisingly, one of the top three benefits of an advisory council mentioned by most presidents and deans was "as a way to involve more people who will give and help with fundraising" (Worth, 2008, p. 18).

Substantive involvement can, indeed, lead to identification with the institution and its priorities. A few years ago I spoke to a gathering of deans at a university on the East Coast. The program for the gathering was my talk and then remarks by a man who was one of the university's major donors. I presented something similar to figure 6.1, answered a few questions, and then turned over the stage to the donor. He began by saying, "That was very interesting because it describes exactly what happened with me—it's interesting to see it from the other perspective." He went on to explain that some years before he had a mild interest in the university; as I recall, he was not an alumnus but had some family connection. Then one day the president called and asked him to attend a meeting with a few other businesspeople to advise the university on a project it was planning. He participated and found the discussion quite interesting, then participated in some follow-up meetings and found his enthusiasm growing. Eventually, the president asked him if he would join the board and he accepted.

One night after a board meeting, he explained, he found himself driving home thinking about the meeting, at which some financial challenges facing the university were discussed. He was talking with his wife about it that evening and she said, "Well, this seems to really concern you. Maybe we need to do something about it." And they made a major gift, the first of many. As reflected in his thoughts driving home and in his conversation with his wife, he had come to *identify* with the institution; its challenges and opportunities had become his own. He had taken ownership as a result of his involvement on the board. As a successful businessman, he was by nature someone who seized opportunities and faced challenges head on. He had the financial ability to resolve his own tension about the university's situation. So his philanthropic initiative was understandable and inevitable.

It is important to emphasize that *making a gift* is itself a form of involvement. It is an action that involves taking some *responsibility* for the institution and it is thus a form of substantive involvement as I have defined it previously. Someone who has committed resources to the college or university has expressed their feeling of identification with its purposes and goals and will generally have a heightened interest and awareness thereafter. With proper stewardship, the first gift begins a cycle of involvement, identification, and investment that grows and deepens over time. For that reason, it is a fundraising axiom that the best prospects are past donors. Few donors will have made their last gift, unless it is a bequest.

CAMPAIGN SOLICITATION STRATEGIES

Fundraising is a blend of science and art. This section summarizes some broad strategies for conducting campaign solicitations—the science part. The next chapter offers suggestions related to the art of fundraising, including cultivation and solicitation visits.

The Annual Fund in the Campaign

The annual fund is integrated within the comprehensive campaign, and the overall campaign goal usually includes a subgoal for the total of annual giving over the defined period of the campaign. In most instances, the president will not be deeply involved in the annual giving program, which employs a combination of mail, phone, Internet, and personal solicitations. Some annual giving programs make extensive use of volunteers. In other development programs, the annual fund is largely staff driven. Gift officers complete a large volume of personal visits to solicit leadership annual gifts, defined by level, often $1,000; $5,000; or more per year. The prospects that they manage are those generally believed to be either not ready or not able to make a major gift, although there may be some who emerge as major gift prospects over the course of the campaign. If an annual fund gift officer identifies such potential, then the relationship with that prospect will be moved to a different level, which may involve the president at an appropriate stage.

The very concept of annual giving is characteristic of higher education. Historically, colleges and universities have asked their donors to make one gift per year for operating support, emphasizing the size of the gift rather than the frequency of giving. Gift clubs, competition among graduating classes, challenge gifts, and other techniques are employed to upgrade annual fund donors to higher levels, in which they are recognized in an annual report or other donor listing. Prospects who do not respond initially are, of course, solicited again, perhaps using different methods (e.g., nonresponse to a mailing may be followed by a phone solicitation). But once the donor responds with a gift, the traditional practice has been to not solicit again until the next cycle of the annual fund the following year.

This approach is in contrast to the way many charitable organizations operate. They often solicit their donors multiple times each year. Indeed, as anyone who is a donor to such an organization knows, a gift may be followed by an acknowledgment that includes another solicitation. Anyone who has made an online gift to a political organization, or some charities, quickly learns to use an e-mail address separate from that at which they receive their everyday business or personal messages, lest their inbox be quickly flooded with resolicitations.

Higher education's approach to annual solicitation reflects the nature of college and university constituencies, which are relatively finite in the short and medium term, including primarily alumni, parents, and others with linkage to the institution, whose relationship is lifelong. The risk of alienating donors through overzealous solicitation is one to be avoided since there are not obvious sources of many new prospects. Charitable and advocacy nonprofits, on the other hand, are constantly renting lists, testing appeals, and discarding names that do not eventually produce revenue. But alumni of a college are alumni forever, and their numbers grow only through the graduation of new classes, the members of which are mostly, by definition, young and years away from their peak giving ability. The situation calls for care in preserving relationships with them.

However, in recent years, some colleges and universities have begun to add a second solicitation to their annual fund programs. For example, donors who give in the fall may be solicited again in the spring for a second gift. Some institutions have found this approach to be successful and a source of significant additional unrestricted revenue (Masterson, 2009).

The second annual fund appeal needs to be handled carefully. It should acknowledge that the individual has already given, offer justification for the second ask, and provide some incentive to give again. Some solicitations

cite the end of a fiscal year (June 30 for many institutions), and the opportunity to upgrade to a higher level gift club before the donor list for the year
is compiled or published, the need for additional gifts to meet a challenge
grant, or perhaps some special need, such as increased scholarship support
in a year of recession and state funding cutbacks. In some cases, a first solicitation may ask for unrestricted support to the institution and the second
for a gift for a specific unit or program, or vice versa.

Again, the president is usually not deeply involved in the annual giving
program, but the overall plan for solicitation, possibly including a second
ask, is one that he or she should understand.

Double and Combined Asks

The annual fund can be neglected in the context of soliciting major commitments to a campaign and the result can be detrimental to the overall
fundraising program. There is the risk that a major gift commitment will
replace the annual gift that the donor would otherwise make; the result
is to shift some money from one of the institution's pockets to another,
often replacing unrestricted support with something that is restricted. For
example, a donor who has been giving $5,000 annually to the annual fund
may be solicited for a $100,000 commitment to the campaign, payable in
five annual installments of $20,000 each. With a $100,000 gift, the likelihood is that the donor will designate some specific purpose, for example,
endowment of a scholarship. However, $25,000 of the endowment is in
reality subsidized by the institution, since it comes from a reduction in annual giving as a result of the donor's gift being shifted to an endowment
purpose.

Common strategies for avoiding this result are the double ask and the
combined ask. The two approaches are somewhat different, although many
people tend to use the terms interchangeably. In a double ask strategy, the
donor in the above example would be asked to commit $100,000 to estab-
lish the scholarship endowment, with the understanding that the annual
fund program will continue to ask for his or her usual annual gift every year
through a separate solicitation. A combined ask builds both purposes of
giving into one commitment, for example, a five-year pledge of $125,000,
which will include $5,000 for the annual fund each year and $20,000 to be
added to the scholarship endowment, which then will total $100,000 (plus
any reinvested earnings) at the conclusion of the pledge.

The virtue of the double ask is that it leaves open the opportunity to upgrade, or increase, the individual's annual gift over the five-year period and,
perhaps, by separating the capital gift from annual giving, maintains the
habit of the annual giving so that it will continue after the campaign pledge
has been paid. The downside is, of course, that the donor may not be clear

about the understanding and will be annoyed by, or will ignore, the annual fund solicitation. The advantage of the combined ask, and pledge, is simplicity and the assurance that the annual fund gift will be maintained, even if at a constant level, over the life of the campaign. The downside is that the annual gift is locked in for the pledge period and there is no opportunity to upgrade it over that time. It would be, of course, possible to build an annual increase in annual fund support into the overall commitment, but that may be more complexity than some donors will embrace.

The combined ask is good practice but, in my experience, sometimes faces some obstacles. Sophisticated donors who are committed to the institution may understand and agree to a combined pledge. Others may not be that attuned to the institution's need for different types of support. They may feel that they are giving as much as they can to the college or university, period, and the details are not of great concern. But, depending on the purpose of the campaign commitment, it may be possible to devise a gift plan that meets both the institution's need for flexible revenue and the donor's desire to direct his or her gift toward a campaign capital priority.

For example, consider the $100,000 donor mentioned earlier, who wishes to create an endowed scholarship fund. If the gift is paid over five years, it might be necessary to wait until the sixth year to award the full scholarship (say for $4,000–$5,000, depending on the endowment payout rate). But the donor may be eager to see scholarships awarded sooner, in order to have the immediate satisfaction of seeing students on campus supported by his or her philanthropy. A reasonable proposal, then, would be a combined gift that permits immediate scholarship awards while also building the endowment to support them in perpetuity. For example, the plan might be something like that illustrated in table 6.1.

Table 6.1. Combined Gift Scholarship Endowment

Based on $125,000 total commitment, five annual installments:					
Year	Total Pledge Payment	Expendable for Current-Year Scholarship Award	Added to Endowment Principal	Endowment Principal Total at Year-End	Endowment Income Expended for Scholarship Award
1	$25,000	$5,000	$20,000	$20,000	-0-
2	$25,000	$5,000	$20,000	$40,000	-0-
3	$25,000	$5,000	$20,000	$60,000	-0-
4	$25,000	$5,000	$20,000	$80,000	-0-
5	$25,000	$5,000	$20,000	$100,000	-0-
6	-0-	-0-	-0-	$100,000	$4,000–5,000

NOTES: Ignores potential growth in endowment principal over the payment period.
Endowment income expended depends on the spending limit adopted by the institution.

Of course, in the plan depicted in table 6.1, the expendable portion of each year's gift is not unrestricted in the way that annual fund gifts may be. But the impact on the institution's budget may be just the same. The gift may reduce the amount of institutional resources that need to be devoted to financial aid and represent, in effect, additional tuition revenue. With careful budgeting and accounting that income can be captured for general operating needs.

One perennial debate on many campuses is the definition of the annual fund. Some institutions follow a very strict definition and count only gifts that are unrestricted at the institutional level, that is, for use at the president's discretion. Others also include gifts that are restricted to benefit a particular unit, but not further restricted as to use; for example, a gift to the engineering school over which the dean has discretion. Grants that support specific projects are expendable for current operations but are generally not considered part of the annual fund, since there is no discretion as to their use and they generally result from efforts other than the annual fund program. Other expendable gifts, for example, those designated for scholarships or broad areas of research, fall into a middle ground, which some may count as annual giving and others may not. But, again, some money is fungible, and gifts of this nature may be just as useful as unrestricted gifts to the annual fund.

Which gifts are counted toward the annual fund is not an unimportant question. The answer may affect the incentives of the annual giving staff and, indeed, the major gifts program as well. If the expendable portion of a pledge like that illustrated in table 6.1 is not included in annual fund totals, the annual fund staff may see the arrangement as detracting from their results. That perception may, over time, lead to destructive internal competition and the withholding of information about prospects, among other dysfunctions.

Planned Giving in the Campaign

Planned giving is an integral part of most comprehensive campaigns. As discussed in chapter 5, exactly how planned gifts of various types are counted toward the campaign goal and how they are reflected in campaign reports is a policy decision that the campaign leadership needs to reach during the planning phase. Consistent with the Council for Advancement and Support of Education's guidelines, campaign reporting should clearly distinguish outright gifts and pledges from planned gifts that are irrevocable (for example, charitable remainder trusts and charitable gift annuities) and planned gifts that are revocable (for example, bequest intentions and charitable remainder trusts that retain the donor's ability to change the charitable beneficiary). But the guidelines provide for some flexibility in how such commitments may be counted toward the campaign goal and in how donors may be recognized.

Some major gifts may be structured to include a combination of outright and planned gifts. Indeed, some experts recommend following a triple-ask strategy, in which prospects are asked to consider an overall campaign commitment that includes the annual fund, a multiyear pledge toward one of the campaign's capital objectives, and a planned gift commitment, which could be unrestricted or restricted to some purpose. This approach may make it possible for the donor to make a larger overall commitment, which adds to campaign momentum and helps raise sights for others, while also establishing a lifelong relationship between the individual and the institution that may lead to further giving in years and campaigns ahead.

For example, the combined gift illustrated in table 6.1 could be expanded to include additional components. The annual income from the endowment created during the campaign, say $4,000–$5,000 (depending on what payout rate may be in effect) might be sufficient to provide, say, 20 percent of tuition for one student. Perhaps the donor wishes to provide such support for five students eventually, perhaps naming the awards to honor or memorialize various members of his or her family. Assuming that the donor is not in a position to give $500,000 outright during the campaign, he or she might proceed with the $125,000 combined gift over five years and also consider a planned gift that will eventually increase the endowment to $500,000. That amount might be sufficient to support four or five scholarships eventually. The planned gift might include irrevocable or revocable arrangements or some combination, depending on the donor's assets and other factors. Of course, the $500,000 is in present dollars, and the date by which the planned gift will be available for addition to the endowment is uncertain, so the gift agreement or memorandum of understanding needs to address the issue of present value and the likely impact of the enhanced scholarship endowment in comparison with what tuition may be in the future.

The discussion in chapter 7 will pick up and elaborate on some of the ideas expressed here, because closing a major gift requires gaining insight into the donor, which involves art in relationships and communication as well as the science of gift planning.

Challenge Gifts

Challenge gifts or grants are a time-tested strategy utilized in both annual fund programs and major gift campaigns. The common principle is that a donor, or donors, makes a commitment to match (either $1-for-$1 or by some other formula) gifts made by others. The purpose is to create an incentive to others who may be attracted by the opportunity to leverage the impact of their support. The implication is that the challenge gift donor will give to match qualifying gifts from others but will not complete the payments if the challenge is not met.

In addition to the opportunity to leverage their gifts, such an arrangement may appeal to donors who would not wish to see their college or university lose an opportunity that is almost within its grasp. The possibility that the institution may not receive the challenge gift may motivate them to participate. The challenge gift is thus a strategy for creating urgency.

Challenge gifts are appropriate and effective, but they can raise both ethical and practical issues. Challenges usually have a time limit (e.g., by the end of the fiscal year) or a cap (e.g., gifts will be matched up to a total of $100,000). There needs to be disclosure if the challenge has been met or the cap has been exceeded. For example, if a one-to-one challenge is capped at $100,000 and it stimulates an additional $120,000 in giving, it is clear that some of the new gifts have not been matched. Of course, if the challenge is not met, there may be appropriate ways of extending or modifying the arrangement to assure that it eventually will be, but that also needs to be done transparently.

In the annual fund, a challenge gift (or grant, if from a company or foundation) is often intended to upgrade gifts, recapture lapsed donors, or acquire new donors. Various formulas for matching are used. For example, figure 6.2 is a report on the Amonette Annual Fund Challenge at Hendrix College. The donors, Dr. Rex A. and Johnnie Amonette, committed to match new and increased gifts to the college's annual fund during the specified fiscal year, an initiative which the college reports was successful in generating additional revenue. Figure 6.3 describes a different type of challenge grant, in which the Hewlett Foundation will match major gifts for the endowment of chairs at the University of California–Berkeley, on a dollar-for-dollar basis. This type of challenge may be especially attractive to donors, since the chair can be named in honor of the individual donor, for a $1.5 million gift. Matched with $1.5 million from Hewlett, that creates a $3 million endowment, the required amount for naming of a distinguished endowed chair at Berkeley. Some state governments also maintain programs that match private gifts for the creation of endowed chairs and professorships along similar lines.

Some challenge gifts, especially in the annual fund arena, include more complex formulas, for example, $2-for-$1 matching of new gifts. But this is an area in which scholars have undertaken research, with useful findings. For example, economists Dean Karlan and John List conducted an experiment using a direct mail solicitation to fifty thousand previous donors to a nonprofit organization. They found that a $1-to-$1 match was effective in increasing both the average gift and the response rate, but that larger match ratios ($3-for-$1 and $2-for-$1) did not have additional impact (Karlan and List, 2007).

HENDRIX COLLEGE: THE AMONETTE
ANNUAL FUND CHALLENGE

Hendrix thanks Dr. Rex A. and Johnnie Amonette '61 and '63 of Memphis, Tenn., for a successful challenge grant! The Amonettes pledged $50,000 to match any new or increased gifts to the Annual Fund before the end of the fiscal year on May 31, 2009. Any gift from someone who did not support the Annual Fund during the 2007–2008 fiscal year or any increase in gifts over the amount given last year qualified for the match.

The Amonettes' dollar-for-dollar challenge inspired 412 donors and raised an additional $109,006 for the College. They issued the challenge because of the difference Hendrix made in their lives; now their challenge has made a difference in the life of the College.

SOURCE: Hendrix College. (N.d.). "The Amonette Annual Fund Challenge." www.hendrix.edu/giving/giving.aspx?id=38835 (accessed July 10, 2009).

Figure 6.2.   Challenge Gift: Annual Fund

WHAT IS THE HEWLETT
FOUNDATION ENDOWED CHAIR CHALLENGE?

The William and Flora Hewlett Foundation has made a landmark $110-million challenge gift to endow 100 new faculty chairs at UC Berkeley. The gift will decisively bolster Berkeley's efforts to retain and recruit top faculty — the heart of the University's excellence. The Hewlett Challenge will match 80 gifts of $1 million to endow 80 new $2-million faculty chairs, each to be located in one of the campus's 14 schools or colleges. It will also match 20 gifts of $1.5 million to endow 20 new $3-million distinguished endowed chairs, which will span multiple academic areas, under the Chancellor's leadership. In all, the Challenge will bring a total of $220 million to reinforce faculty excellence across the campus.

SOURCE: University of California–Berkeley. (N.d.). "About the Challenge." hewlettchallenge.berkeley.edu/about/ (accessed July 10, 2009).

Figure 6.3.   University of California–Berkeley: Hewlett Foundation Endowed Chair Challenge

Challenge gifts can be overused. If a challenge is always in effect, it no longer creates urgency because it is just the norm. The challenge needs to be credible. There are examples of challenges that are said to be from an anonymous donor, or a group of anonymous donors, or from the board of trustees as a group. In my opinion, these arrangements are not sufficiently credible; a cynical person might suspect that they are just made up. I prefer a challenge like that at Hendrix College, shown in figure 6.1, in which the challenge gift donors are identified by name; indeed, the college's website includes their photos and a description of their relationship with the college. People are more likely to respond to a challenge from real people, with names and faces, or from a prestigious foundation like Hewlett, than from anonymous and possibly fictitious groups of people.

The Solicitation Team

Chapter 7 discusses techniques of solicitation, but at the strategic level the formula for success is well established: having the right person (or persons) ask the right person for the right gift at the right time. Especially for the leadership gifts at the top of the gift chart, the composition of the solicitation team, the amount and purpose of the ask, and the timing of the solicitation should be matters of very thoughtful consideration.

Some solicitations may be conducted one-on-one, but it will often be more effective to involve a team of two, perhaps a volunteer leader and the president/dean/director/chief development officer. As my campaign anecdote recounted in chapter 3 illustrates, it is often useful to include a volunteer leader, who brings credibility and personal example to the discussion, as well as a staff officer of the institution, who may have more detailed knowledge about programs and the campaign.

One question that frequently arises is the point in the cultivation/solicitation process at which the president should be involved. I have known presidents who hold the view that their scare time should be primarily allocated to closing, that is, they would prefer not to visit a prospect until previous contacts by staff have moved that prospect to the point of readiness to make the gift. The president then makes the ask and is all but assured of a positive response. But, in practice, that is not always realistic.

Indeed, the process often may work the other way around. Some prominent prospects may not be receptive to staff visits but may be flattered by the request for a meeting from a president or a dean. In this case, the president or dean may be needed to open the door with a prospect, after which he or she will be receptive to follow-up discussions with a chief development officer or other professional. That follow up is greatly facilitated if the president has included the development officer in the visit. That establishes the personal contact between the prospect and the development officer and empowers the development officer as an agent of the president and the institution. He or she then can follow up with the prospect on the president's behalf. To invoke chapter 3's football metaphor, in the latter case the president is a blocker who opens the hole through which a runner may gain yardage and advance the ball.

Determination of the solicitation team needs to be based on an objective assessment of which combination of individuals is most likely to be effective with the prospect. Considerations of internal politics and egos should be avoided. That is not always easy, especially in universities where some may feel protective of their relationships with donors and fear that discussions with a prospect may lead to a diversion of the gift away from their particular priorities. To be frank, there also can be situations in which more than one person wants to receive credit (perhaps in the eyes of a supervisor or the faculty) for having obtained the gift and thus wants to be a member of the solicitation team. Accommodating such concerns can lead to a mismatch of solicitors with prospects and solicitation teams that are too large.

Early in my career at the University of Maryland–College Park, it was my responsibility as the director of development to assemble a team for an important visit to solicit a major gift. Because I was relatively new in the job, and still relatively early on my professional learning curve, I set up the appointment and then asked five people to attend, including the campus chancellor, the president of the university system, the vice president for development of the university system, the director of the program for which the gift was sought, and the dean of the school to whom that director reported. Plus me, that makes six! (More than a basketball team, but at least less than a football team.) I do not recall that any of those individuals had a burning desire to participate in the meeting—this was not so much a matter of internal politics or ego—but rather overzealousness on my part. I wanted every key player to be there for this important solicitation. I thought I was being thorough and that the prospect would be impressed by the firepower I had delivered to his office that day. I could see surprise on his face as the invading army entered his office; extra chairs needed to be carried in from the waiting area and a table needed to be moved aside to accommodate us. As it turned out, the meeting went well and the prospect concluded by saying he would consider his decision. He called me a few days later to say that he had decided to make the gift. "I will rely on you to inform the others," he said. With a smile in his voice, he added, "But I don't need all of them coming over together to thank me personally."

CAMPAIGN MANAGEMENT METRICS

Campaign progress must be monitored throughout, both to assure that milestones are achieved and to identify areas of underperformance that may require adjustments to the plan. The metrics most relevant to a particular institution or campaign will, of course, vary, but some top-level indicators might include

- progress toward the overall dollar goal, in terms of commitments;
- progress toward subgoals for specific campaign objectives, academic units, and so on;
- progress by gift levels, that is, in relation to the gift range chart;
- progress by types of commitments, that is, current and deferred, revocable and irrevocable;
- commitments and gifts by source, that is, alumni, other individuals, corporations, foundations;
- history and projections of cash flow, that is, annual fund, pledge fulfillment, planned gifts; and
- campaign budget performance and projections.

In addition to monitoring financial reports, a president may wish to review summary reports concerning campaign activity, including the performance of campaign staff. Individual staff member performance should be the responsibility of the chief development officer, but the president and the campaign leadership committee may find it useful to monitor such metrics as

- number of cultivation, solicitation, follow-up, and stewardship visits completed;
- numbers of prospects in various stages of the cultivation cycle;
- number of letters of inquiry and proposals submitted to foundations and corporations;
- alumni participation in annual giving; and
- advancement services summary data, for example, research reports completed, accurate database records maintained, gift acknowledgment turn around time.

Again, evaluation of individual staff performance is best delegated to the chief development officer or campaign director, but the metrics by which such performance will be measured and what incentives may be offered to campaign staff are policy questions in which the president should be involved.

The measurement and evaluation of development staff performance, especially those with responsibility for major gifts, is a topic worthy of discussion that goes beyond the scope of this book. But there are a few key principles to be considered.

First, performance should be measured by more than dollars raised. Gifts and commitments are, of course, the ultimate purpose of all development activity, and most systems for evaluating development staff include dollar goals at least in part. But measuring performance by that standard alone raises several issues. It is often difficult to fully attribute credit for a single gift to one individual; many players may have been involved with a prospect over time, and all may have helped to bring that donor to the point of a gift. Attributing the outcome to the work of one staff member has the potential to undermine teamwork and communication, creating dysfunction that is detrimental to the overall campaign. Using the dollar bottom line as the sole measure of development officer performance also may create an incentive to emphasize the immediate gift, rather than take a longer term perspective that may be in the institution's ultimate best interests. And, of course, too much pressure to close gifts, especially if the fund raiser's compensation is related to the bottom line, could raise the possibility of ethical concerns, for example, misleading donors or misrepresenting the institution in some way.

Second, performance measures need to reflect the individual's job description. Some staff members who have responsibility for major gifts fundraising also have administrative, management, or communications roles that will occupy some portion of their time; others do not. Performance measures need to be varied accordingly.

And, third, performance needs to be measured in relationship to the donor constituency that the development officer manages. For example, gift officers working in the annual fund would generally be expected to complete more solicitation visits than those working with major gift prospects, since the latter will be engaged in more cultivation activity. The metrics for foundation relations professionals may not emphasize personal visits, to which foundation officials may be generally unreceptive; the number of letters, proposals, and reports prepared may be better measures of productive efforts, and some portion of time spent internally learning about academic programs and faculty research perhaps should be credited as well.

Colleges and universities have various standards by which they evaluate their development officers, and evolving models are topics of discussion at professional conferences. One model, developed by Richard J. Dupree, executive director of development at Indiana University's Kelley School of Business, is shown in table 6.2. The model was developed for the Corporation for Public Broadcasting but some version of it has been adopted by a number of higher education institutions and nonprofit organizations.

Table 6.2.   Dupree's Major Gift Officer Evaluation Standards

	Points
Dollar goal (cash and pledges)	25
Proposals submitted	25
Contacts	25
Quality of work	25
A. "Hit rate"	5
B. Prospecting	5
C. Cultivations	5
D. Use of management/leadership	5
E. Budget management	5
TOTAL	100

SOURCE: Dupree, Richard K. (N.d.). *Measuring Performance: A Station Manager's Guide to Evaluating Major Gift Officers.* majorgivingnow.org/downloads/pdf/dupree.pdf (accessed July 16, 2009).

This tool includes five indices of performance based on a total possible one hundred points. Achievement of a dollar goal, based both on cash and pledges, accounts for twenty-five points, but dollars are not the sole measure of the gift officer's performance. Additional points can be earned through other productive activity, including the submission of proposals, contacts with prospects, and five sub-indicators that measure quality of work. The latter provide incentives for identifying new prospects, engaging in cultivation, and involving institutional officers in fundraising. Some weighting of metrics is appropriate and avoids perverse incentives. For example, if dollar totals were the only measure, a development officer might aggressively solicit gifts and ignore the identification and cultivation of new prospects necessary to maintain a pipeline. Or, the development officer might get lucky with a big gift early in the year and then coast for the balance of the time. But, in Dupree's model, even in the event of such a windfall, he or she would still need to be active to meet the other goals, for contacts, proposals submitted, and so forth. On the other hand, a gift officer who shows intense activity in contacting donors still cannot be successful without closing some gifts. That requires that he or she focus on prospects who are ready to give and not just engage in repeated contacts with individuals who are not major prospects or who are unlikely to give in the near term.

Dupree recommends that a major gifts officer earn at least seventy-five points to be considered satisfactory. A warning (and potentially eventual termination) would be appropriate if he or she achieves less than seventy-five. The gift officer might be paid a bonus if he or she achieves more than eighty points (Hall, 2006). The subject of bonuses for fundraising performance is controversial. But incentive compensation can meet ethical standards, so long as the payment is not a percentage of funds raised and especially if the metrics include activity rather than just dollars committed.

Again, the president should not be involved in the evaluation of individual development staff members, but he or she should be a part of the discussion regarding the methodology to be applied and be comfortable that it represents sound policy. The president and campaign committee may also wish to review summary data on staff activity in the course of the campaign, but not at the level of individuals.

REFERENCES

Dunlop, David R. (2002). "Major Gift Programs." In Michael J. Worth (Ed.), *New Strategies for Educational Fund Raising*. Westport, CT: American Council on Education and Praeger, pp. 89–104.

Hall, Holly. (2006). "Evaluating How a Fund Raiser Does in Luring Big Gifts" [electronic version]. *Chronicle of Philanthropy*, March 23, pp. 1–3. www.kelley.iu.edu/newswire/img/052006/cparticle.pdf (accessed July 16, 2006).

Karlan, Dean, and John A. List. (2007). "Does Price Matter in Charitable Giving? Evidence from a Large-Scale Natural Field Experiment." *American Economic Review* 97, no. 5 (December), pp. 1774–1793. www.aeaweb.org/articles.php?doi=10.1257/aer.97.5.1774 (accessed July 10, 2009).

Kelly, Kathleen S. (1998). *Effective Fund Raising Management*. Mahwah, NJ: Lawrence Erlbaum Associates.

Masterson, Kathryn. (2009). "Thanks for Your Generosity: Now Can You Give Again?" *Chronicle of Higher Education* 55, no. 38 (June 22). chronicle.com/article/Thanks-for-Your-Generosity/44241/ (accessed July 10, 2009).

Rosso, Henry A. (2003). *Achieving Excellence in Fund Raising*. 2nd edition. Edited by Eugene R. Tempel. San Francisco: Jossey-Bass.

Seiler, Timothy L. (2003). "Plan to Succeed." In Henry A. Rosso, *Achieving Excellence in Fund Raising* (2nd edition), edited by Eugene R. Tempel. San Francisco: Jossey-Bass, pp. 23–29.

Smith, G. T. (1977). "The Development Program." In A. W. Rowland (Ed.), *Handbook of Institutional Advancement*. San Francisco: Jossey-Bass, pp. 142–151.

Worth, Michael J. (2008). *Sounding Boards: Advisory Councils in Higher Education*. Washington, DC: Association of Governing Boards of Universities and Colleges.

7

The Art of Fundraising

This chapter offers some practical principles and recommendations for presidents, deans, development officers, and other campus leaders in cultivating relationships with donors and in soliciting gifts. It is titled "The Art of Fundraising" because it concerns those aspects of fundraising that involve primarily insight, intuition, and judgment. First, it clarifies different types of gifts and the place of cultivation and solicitation in pursuing each, then discusses the motivations of major gift donors and strategies for engaging them. Finally, it provides recommendations for successful solicitation visits.

Since this activity is by definition an "art," the chapter relies extensively on my own experience and observation. Some may, of course, disagree with my suggestions and prefer to approach the subject in a different way. That is, of course, quite fine. There is no one right way to make art.

TYPES OF GIFTS AND SITUATIONS

Fundraising is different under various circumstances; how it is approached depends on the type of gift that is sought and how that type of gift fits into the donor's overall pattern of giving. David Dunlop (2002) identifies three types of gifts that individuals make, and styles of fundraising that are practiced in relationship to each. The distinctions are centrally important to the discussion of cultivation and solicitation, which receive different emphases in each of these approaches.

According to Dunlop, most people make regular gifts to selected causes and institutions with which they are involved or have affinity, including perhaps a college or university, a church, charitable organizations that serve their community, and those that pursue important causes, such as the environment. These gifts may be made annually or more frequently and are usually made from the donor's disposable income. In higher education, these are usually made to the annual fund. Dunlop identifies the style of fundraising that solicits regular (or annual) gifts as "speculative." That does not imply risk, but rather an approach that emphasizes volume, and that includes many solicitations with little or no cultivation on the front end, based on the speculation that some percentage will result in gifts.

College and university presidents are not usually involved very much in this type of fundraising. It is usually conducted through the annual fund program, using mail, phone, the Internet, and other methods, as well as personal solicitations that may be undertaken by volunteers or paid staff. Presidents may be practicing this style of fundraising when they speak to a large group with a general encouragement of giving. They are, in effect, speculating that their words will find a positive reception in some percentage of ears. But presidents are not usually involved in direct solicitations in this mode.

A second type of giving Dunlop labels as "special gifts" (Dunlop, 2002). Special gifts are made to address some special need of the institution, for example, in response to a campaign. The timing reflects not the calendar, but the institution's priorities and plans. Special gifts are usually major gifts; they are larger than annual gifts and are usually paid over a period of years. Often they are made from the donor's assets rather than income, although that may not always be the case. The related approach to fundraising is, in Dunlop's phrase, "campaign or project fundraising." In this mode of fundraising, Dunlop estimates, about one-half of the time is dedicated to cultivation and about one-half dedicated to solicitation. In other words, some time must be expended to develop the relationship with the prospect and make the case for the major gift, but in a campaign, there is also urgency about moving to the solicitation and closing the gift (or moving on).

The third type of gift, referenced earlier in this book, is what Dunlop calls the "ultimate gift." It is the largest gift of which the donor is capable, often made from the donor's assets or estate, and sometimes directed to an institution's endowment. It is often, although not always, made later in a person's life or upon death. The appropriate style of fundraising is the "nurturing" approach, which may include 90 percent or more cultivation of the relationship—over a period of years—and 10 percent or less solicitation. Indeed, as Dunlop (2002) observes, such gifts may never actually be solicited. Rather, they evolve from a lifelong relationship between an institution and a donor.

Although Dunlop (2002) calls the second approach "campaign fundraising," today's comprehensive campaigns really operate in all three modes simultaneously. The annual fund goes on continuously. The speculative approach—relying on the volume of solicitations to produce the needed revenue—is still the norm in the annual fund, but technology also has made it possible to engage in more personalized cultivation and stewardship of annual fund prospects and donors. Indeed, the application of marketing principles and communications technology has led to some convergence of marketing and fundraising practice in this area.

As discussed in chapter 6 and elsewhere in this book, campaigns do create pressure to close, but they do not preclude the nurturing approach to fundraising with at least a selected number of prospects. Moreover, most campaigns continue for so long and are so frequent that many institutions are engaged in the continuous cultivation of relationships with donors, some of whom may make their ultimate gifts in response to today's campaign and some of whom may do so in a subsequent campaign. The emphasis on planned giving has indeed encouraged continuity in relationships with donors over the long haul.

But the heart of most campaigns remains the major, or special, gift. The campaign goal and deadline drive the process and require a balance between cultivation and solicitation activity. The discussion in this chapter is primarily set in this mode. It assumes that the purpose is to identify, cultivate, and solicit a prospect within the time frame of the campaign and suggests some techniques for pursuing that end effectively.

As discussed in chapter 3, the most effective fundraising requires a partnership of volunteer leaders, the president and other academic officers, and the development professionals. The importance of volunteer involvement and the unique contributions that such leaders bring to solicitations were discussed there and emphasized as well in other sections of this book. But the reality in many campaigns is that presidents and deans and other campus leaders may need to take the lead in a large number of solicitations. The volume of contacts required to achieve campaign goals, especially in the middle levels of the gift range chart, may require that presidents and their chief development officers be the team on many cultivation and solicitation visits. It is perhaps desirable, but not always feasible, to involve a volunteer in every such event. This chapter is addressed primarily to presidents regarding their own fundraising and not so much to volunteers. Some points may be relevant as well to volunteer solicitors, but their relationship with prospects is different from that of campus officials.

GETTING IN THE RIGHT MIND-SET

The first step in preparing for fundraising starts inside the fund raiser's own head. Getting in the right mind-set requires holding an understanding of fundraising and philanthropy as positive and noble activities, rather than negative or exploitative ones; framing the relationship between the solicitor and the prospect; and understanding the motivations of major gift donors, that is, seeing the interaction from the donor's point of view. The following sections discuss these three requirements. Some of the discussion draws on insights from the fundraising literature, but some also represents insights and opinions based on my own observation and experience.

The Nature of Fundraising and Giving

I have worked with presidents and deans who are naturally excellent fund raisers. They approach the task with enthusiasm and ease and relish the opportunity to cultivate and solicit gifts to advance their visions and goals for their institutions. I have also known others who find it at least mildly uncomfortable.

The latter is understandable. Although there are an increasing number of presidents who have served as development officers or who have come from careers outside higher education, most presidents still are academics, at least at heart. For most, fundraising was not exactly a career choice made in grade school. Most entered higher education motivated by intellectual values and entered administration to advance educational goals. Most are grounded in the culture of the academy. Important relationships have been with students or faculty colleagues, which usually involve providing nurture, encouragement, and support rather than anything with a self-serving purpose. Entering a meeting with a donor prospect with an end in mind may feel quite different from talking with a student to discuss his or her academic and career goals or with a faculty colleague about his or her research. Again many presidents, deans, and other academic officers relish fundraising, especially with successful experience, but there are others for whom it is a somewhat unnatural activity, at least initially.

The discussion here relates primarily to relationships with individual donors. Many people are quite comfortable soliciting support from a foundation or a corporation, where giving is institutionalized and the person receiving the solicitation is often also a professional. It is, after all, not their personal money and so the solicitation of a gift is not burdened by the concern that making it might impose any sacrifice by the donor. But soliciting an individual donor is emotionally more complicated. It may seem like asking someone to sacrifice something, even if that something is modest in relationship to the person's wealth. Unlike an impersonal foundation or corporation, the funds could presumably be used for some other purpose of benefit to the individual or his or her family. So asking individuals for gifts just presents more psychological barriers.

If a fund raiser perceives cultivation as manipulative or solicitation as merely transactional—a game in which the solicitor is the hunter and the prospect the prey—it is understandable that any good person would hesitate. Sometimes the language of fundraising may create such perceptions. For example, measuring major gift officer performance in part by their "hit rates," while consistent with the prevailing jargon, does set a tone more appropriate to war—or even football—than to philanthropy.

But a negative understanding of fundraising does not reflect the situation as donors perceive it. Individuals who are not philanthropic and who do not wish to be solicited will self-select out of the process by denying appointments or expressing their lack of interest at an early stage. So, by definition, those with whom the president or other fund raiser is interacting usually will have a positive view of the process and participate with interest. And, as I wrote in chapter 6, I have never known a major donor who regretted making the gift or who did not derive personal satisfaction from the decision. For many donors, becoming associated with a worthwhile and admired institution of higher education is among the most rewarding and fulfilling experiences of their lives. When we ask them to participate, we are not prodding them to painful action but rather offering them an opportunity to experience that reward. As expressed by Frank H. T. Rhodes, former president of Cornell University,

> Universities are one of the glories of civilization. . . . To solicit funds [for them] is not to go, cap-in-hand, begging support for some marginal activity. It is, instead, to invite a friend to share in the privilege of the greatest partnership of all—the quest for knowledge, on which our present existence and our future well-being depend. (Rhodes, 1997, p. xxiv)

Framing Donor Relationships

Presidents and other campus officers develop and maintain relationships with major gift donors, including the volunteers who also work alongside them in the campaign. The cultivation of relationships is at the heart of major gifts fundraising, and it is often the president who is the principal actor with many donors. But the relationships to be cultivated and sustained are those between the donor and the institution. Officials of a college or university who interact with donors do so as *agents* of the institution. The interactions are undertaken with the purpose of advancing the institution's agenda—during and beyond a president's own tenure. That is not to say that such relationships are or should be exploitative or disingenuous—they certainly should not be. Nor do I intend to say that relationships should not be friendly and filled with warmth, consideration, and real feeling. They may indeed evolve to real friendship. But that friendship exists in the context of the institution, the institution's agenda must remain primary, and I think it is important to keep this distinction consciously in mind.

The "problem" with personal friendship is that it can come to be valued above all else. If some line is not maintained, the desire to preserve a personal relationship could inhibit the purposeful and deliberate cultivation of a relationship on the institution's behalf. The desire to maintain a friendship also may make it difficult to walk away from a relationship that is not productive for the institution. The other problem with personal friendship, in this arena, is that it is not easily transferable.

Most presidents do not serve their institutions for a lifetime. Indeed, there may be a change in presidential leadership within the period of a campaign. But many donors do maintain relationships with their colleges and universities for a lifetime and across multiple campaigns. It is highly unusual for a donor to follow a president, or a development officer, to another institution should he or she move—suggesting how donors tend to define and frame such relationships.

It is essential, therefore, to build relationships between donors and the institution that involve multiple people and connections, including campus staff as well as trustees and other volunteers, so that there can be continuity over the years, despite changes in the identity of the principal custodian of the donor-institution relationship.

MOTIVATIONS OF MAJOR DONORS

Getting in the right mind-set for fundraising requires some insight on the motivations of those who make major gifts. The subject of donor motivation has a large literature, including the reflections of fundraising practitioners over many decades and, in more recent years, a growing body of academic research. Some of the research has methodological issues that influence results; for example, asking people why they give is likely to elicit appropriate answers. Some studies relate to philanthropy broadly and are more relevant to nonprofit organizations than to higher education institutions. But some principles emerge consistently in both the practitioner and research literature and offer important insights to educational fund raisers. A full review of the literature on this subject is well beyond the scope of this book, but the following paragraphs include a brief discussion, drawing on some authors and researchers as well as my own observations and reflections.

Seven Faces

One study that provides some useful tools was conducted by Russ Prince and Karen File and published in a 1994 book entitled *The Seven Faces of*

Philanthropy. Although the study is more than a decade old and some have criticized the research methodology used, the conclusions have an intuitive appeal and coincide with some of my own observations over the years. It places major donors into seven distinct categories based on their needs, motivations, and the benefits they receive from giving.

Prince and File acknowledge that there are few pure types, that is, most donors have mixed motives. But many follow primarily one approach or another and are predominant among donors to certain categories of organizations and institutions. (Their study was not limited to higher education donors.)

About 26 percent of the donors studied by Prince and File (1994) were what they characterized as "communitarians." These are individuals motivated by the responsibilities of citizenship in their communities and who might be found among the principal donors to local hospitals, community-based nonprofits, the local United Way, and other causes, in which they participate along with others. Higher education institutions may attract their support if the college or university has a clear importance to the local community and its economy. For example, small business owners, who are often among this category of donor, may support a local community college in the same way as they might support the local YMCA or Boys and Girls Club. But, clearly, donors who are motivated primarily in this way may be less inclined to support elite national institutions or those located far away from their homes.

The second category identified by Prince and File are the "devout," about 21 percent of those in their study. As the term suggests, these individuals give as a manifestation of their religious faith. They support churches, synagogues, or mosques and faith-based nonprofit organizations. They may also support church-related educational institutions associated with their religious denomination. Again, none of these categories are mutually exclusive, so devout donors may also support secular institutions. But it is a category of donor found most commonly among those who give to religious congregations, denominations, and related organizations.

"Investors" were 15 percent of the donors studied by Prince and File. In the Prince and File description, investor-donors are those who approach the gift as a transaction. For example, they may request detailed information on how the funds will be used, what recognition will be provided, and other details of the gift. They encompass but are not synonymous with what we today call entrepreneurial donors or venture philanthropists, whose visibility and impact on philanthropy have emerged since the late 1990s (after the Prince and File research). Investors may comprise a larger portion of donors today than in the mid-1990s, and they present some challenges for higher education, as will be discussed further below.

"Socialites" were about 11 percent of the donors in this study. The term sounds pejorative but is not intended that way. These are donors whose giving is often tied to social activities and relationships. They are prominent in fundraising for the arts, where gifts are often made in connection with performances and other events, and in other types of nonprofits that use black-tie dinners, charity auctions, and similar events as a primary fundraising method. Social standing and prestige in their communities are among the rewards that these donors receive for their participation.

Smaller numbers of donors are found in the Prince and File categories of "altruist" (about 9 percent) and "dynast" (about 8 percent). The former give because it is the "right thing to do" and often support social and political causes; the latter give to institutions based on family traditions.

A type of donor that Prince and File found to be common in support of higher education institutions and hospitals are "re-payers," representing over 10 percent of the donors they studied. These are individuals who support institutions that have provided some important benefit in their own lives or to their families and to which they feel some debt, which they repay through their giving.

As I said earlier, I find Prince and File's donor types to be a useful model to bear in mind. Again, no individual falls exclusively into one category or another, and the list of donor types may not be exhaustive, but in my experience, many exhibit some tendency toward one approach or another. Both as a university development officer and as a consultant who has interviewed donors, I sometimes have been able to gain a sense of an individual's approach to giving by thinking about Prince and File's seven faces. Some of these types are more naturally inclined to support higher education than are others, but often a discussion about a college or university can be guided in a direction most consistent with the approach that the person takes in his or her overall giving.

When I was director of development at the University of Maryland–College Park, I found there were many donors who revealed the perspectives of re-payers. For example, it was common for alumni to tell me that they had been the first in their families to attend college. They would speak of their gratitude for the opportunity the state university had provided them to obtain an affordable education that led to a successful career. Many expressed a desire to give back for the opportunities they had been granted—both to the institution and to the current generation of students. This is not surprising, since state universities historically have been a source of opportunity for young citizens of their states and have produced many self-made successful people.

But I also met Maryland donors who approached their giving with one of the other Prince and File (1994) perspectives. For example, some businesspeople, whether alumni or not, would express a communitarian perspective. They viewed the university as a resource important to the economy of the state and region and would support it primarily for that reason. And, of course, there were others who approached giving with the investor style and a few who were dynasts; they gave to continue a tradition that perhaps their fathers or grandfathers had initiated.

As vice president at The George Washington University (GW), I also met many re-payers. GW is an urban university, located in downtown Washington, DC, and in its earlier history enrolled a substantially part-time student body. It offered many evening programs that provided opportunities for many students who were also employed, many in the agencies of the federal government. A common story would be something like this: "I came to Washington after World War II and got a job working for the government. I rode the trolley to GW after work every night and completed my (law degree/business degree/master's degree) as a part-time student. I am where I am today because of the flexibility and support that GW and its professors provided to me during those years. I owe something to the university to pay it back for what it gave to me."

One GW donor who expressed the desire to re-pay made an especially strong impression on me. He had committed a gift toward one of our campaign objectives, the renovation of a plaza in the center of the campus. I do not recall by whom or exactly how his gift was solicited, but he had made the commitment and my role was to talk with him about recognition. The conversation centered on possible naming of one of the new gates that were being constructed to lead into the plaza. I suggested it might bear his name. "No," he said, "I don't care about seeing my own name. But I have an idea." He explained that he had come to the United States as a child from Cuba with his parents. He received an education and became highly successful. "For me," he said, "the concept of a gateway has a special meaning. Coming to America and attending the university were my gateways to a better life for my family. Let's call it 'America's Gate' to remind people of what education and this country represent." I was, and remain, quite moved by the idea. Together we wrote some words that were engraved on a plaque erected on a column next to the gate and that capture the sentiments he expressed. Having been born and raised in the United States, I found that his experience and words caused me to reflect more deeply on the values of our country. I continue to do so whenever I walk past America's Gate.

At GW, I also heard expressions of gratitude from former patients of the university's medical center, who felt an obligation to give back and to provide for others who would follow them, in exchange for the excellent care that they or members of their family had received. Re-payers were common among donors to the university and its medical center, and I could usually identify that theme early in a conversation. But there also were donors who reflected other Prince and File (1994) perspectives and discussions could be guided accordingly.

It is, of course, never appropriate to mislead or, obviously, to lie to a donor prospect. But it is entirely appropriate to emphasize points with which the donor may especially resonate and to deemphasize those that may not be a good fit with his or her perspectives. For example, in the case of Maryland or GW, when I met a donor who expressed the sentiments of a re-payer, I would reinforce those values. I might talk about the continuing need for scholarships for students who are seeking opportunities today. With a donor who especially valued opportunity for students, I might not devote too much time to boasting about the rising national rankings of the university's research programs or increasing selectivity in its undergraduate admissions (although both were occurring at both Maryland and GW during the years that I represented them). Those are just themes that might not be especially important to a re-payer type of donor and could even raise the question of whether the institution had diverged from that aspect of its mission that the donor most values.

On the other hand, I also met many donors who were of the investor style with regard to their philanthropy. Their questions made it clear that they were concerned with performance and what impact their gifts might have. They sometimes viewed the university from a business perspective and would ask about its strategic plan or its competitive position in one field or another. In those situations, increased research rankings and student qualifications might be exactly the right data to emphasize. It would assure the donor that the university was making measurable progress and that his or her gift would enjoy a solid return on investment.

With donors whose conversation suggested a communitarian approach, I might tilt toward discussing the economic and community impact of the university—in the case of Maryland, its importance to economic and business growth in the state, and with GW, the university's position as the largest private employer and one of the largest providers of medical care in the District of Columbia. An investment in the institution would thus be an investment in the community and the region. Of course, communitarians based in other regions of the country would present a different situation. Their conversations might turn to the needs of local institutions in their home communities, which might be the highest priority for their charitable giving. My approach would be to acknowledge the importance of their local concerns and giving, while also exploring ways to increase their interest in the university.

With altruist donors I might discuss the fundamental importance of research and education to human and social progress and the importance of universities as institutions. With dynasts, the conversation might emphasize the importance of tradition. The donors that Prince and File (1994) identify as socialites are sometimes a challenge for colleges and universities because higher education is not event driven. But there could be linkages with a university's arts programs, or the donors might find it interesting to know more about the university's gift clubs and the social events in which members are entitled to participate.

Again, to emphasize, it is a mistake to stereotype people, and no donor neatly fits into one or another of Prince and File's (1994) seven faces—most people are complex in their approaches to institutions and to giving. And I do not think these types are exhaustive of all donors. But the seven faces do offer some insight and can be a convenient set of frames for gaining an initial understanding of a donor's motivation and then guiding the conversation to points that might be especially consistent with his or her values.

Cajoling versus Inclination

Among productive scholars on the motivations of major donors is Paul Schervish, a sociologist and director of Boston College's Center on Wealth and Philanthropy. Schervish's research, much of it undertaken with his colleague John Havens, has focused on the philanthropic motivations of high net–worth individuals. Schervish's work provides not only insights on donors (what he calls the "supply side"), but also an approach for fund raisers (the "demand side").

Schervish and Havens (2002) identify six principal motivations of wealthy donors, including hyperagency, identification, association, tax aversion, death, and gratitude. Hyperagency is the history-making capacity of wealthy individuals, that is, their "enhanced capacity . . . to control the conditions under which they and others live," in other words, to change the world (p. 225). The term "identification" has a somewhat different meaning in Schervish and Havens's writing than it does in the Five I's (discussed in chapter 6). These authors mean the donor's identification with the needs of others, which they think increases from association with those people, rather than identification with an institution. But the concepts are related. Gratitude as a motivation is consistent with the values of the re-payers identified by Prince and File (1994). Tax aversion and death (or the contemplation thereof) may affect the size, structure, and timing of a gift more than comprising an underlying motivation. Thus, while Schervish and Havens make a contribution to understanding donor motivation, their findings do not radically depart from what others have observed.

Where their work breaks ground is in their critique of traditional fundraising and the suggestion of a different approach to cultivation and solicitation. It is related to the discussion earlier in this chapter concerning the solicitor's mind-set.

Traditional fundraising, they argue, sometimes takes a "cajoling" or "scolding" approach. In this approach, fundraisers begin with the assumption that donors need to be persuaded to be generous. Fund raisers proceeding with this assumption "present needs, arouse a sense of obligation, offer psychological inducements, and otherwise animate the forces at their disposal to impress upon wealth holders their duty to supply charitable gifts" (Schervish and Havens, 2002, p. 223). The authors acknowledge that in practice this approach is "only on occasion enunciated or exercised so severely . . . and it is seldom carried out without some complementary attention to a donor's intent and inclination" (p. 223). Nevertheless, they argue, the cajoling model is based on faulty assumptions about donor motivation. Wealthy individuals are *inclined* toward philanthropy, and Schervish and Havens recommend an approach to fundraising that acknowledges and capitalizes on that reality. It is a donor-centered approach that they call the "inclination model" (pp. 224, 231). It is, they write, more like marketing than sales. In this approach, the fund raiser guides the prospect to consider four questions:

1. Is there something you want to do with your wealth?
2. That fulfills the needs of others?
3. That you can do more efficiently and more effectively than government or commercial enterprise?
4. And that expands your personal happiness by enabling you to express your gratitude and actualize your identification with the fate of others? (Schervish and Havens, 2002, p. 225)

The goal, according to Schervish and Havens (2002), is to locate "the point of convergence between the donor's need for effectiveness and significance and the prospects of those in need" (p. 231). In other words, this is an approach to matching the donor's interests to the needs and priorities of the institution. That is not exactly a new idea in fundraising, and it is reflected in my previous discussion of the Prince and File (1994) donor types. But the recommendations to begin with a donor-centered approach and tone, to listen more than talk, and to enter the conversation with positive assumptions about the generosity and noble intentions of donor prospects are all sound. That is especially true with today's sophisticated donors, appropriate in an environment of competition for philanthropy, and consistent with the values of educational institutions.

Donor-Centered Approach

The questions actually presented in a visit with a prospect likely would not be exactly the words that Schervish and Havens (2002) suggest. But an effective fund raiser guides the conversation with a prospect through questions that may cover similar ground.

For example, during a prospect visit I might, after an appropriate period of small talk, initiate a transition in the conversation by asking, "How did you decide to attend [name of university]? Looking back, do you think it was a good choice?" The answers may reveal a potential re-payer or some other important insight on the individual's feelings about the institution. At a later point, I might guide the conversation closer to the target by asking, "So, what are your volunteer and philanthropic interests?" The question presumes that the individual has some, which most do, but it often invites further reflection. A good follow-up might be, "Why are those causes/organizations important to you?" This path may lead ultimately to something like, "What aspects of the university's work do you think might be closest to your goals for your philanthropy?" Again, the presumption is that there is a match and the hope is that the prospect may identify at least a general territory in which the point of convergence may be found. This chapter will return to the topic of technique in cultivation and solicitation visits again below, but first, there are some additional points that need to be explored regarding donor motivation.

Entrepreneurial Donors

Schervish's concept of hyperagency and the donor-centered approach raise questions for higher education fund raisers: What if the donor goes to a place that the college or university does not want to go? What if his or her interests just do not coincide with the priorities of higher education? Or what if the donor has ideas for a gift to the college or university that it would be inadvisable to accept? In other words, are the trends toward entrepreneurial donors and venture philanthropy ones that work against colleges and universities? Or are there ways in which the inclinations and style of such donors can be accommodated by higher education institutions?

As with the topic of donor motivation generally, an extensive literature has developed around these questions. It includes an award-winning doctoral dissertation written by Luisa Boverini at the University of Pennsylvania, summarized in her article in the *International Journal of Educational Advancement* in 2006, and numerous other writings that describe efforts by universities to engage entrepreneurial donors.

The terms "venture philanthropy," "entrepreneurial donor," "high-engagement philanthropy," "high-impact philanthropy," and others are often used interchangeably, although there are some distinctions. The fine points are not essential to this discussion, and the concepts have similarities.

Entrepreneurial donors are often relatively young, although those who started in the tech boom of the 1990s are showing some gray hair. Most achieved their wealth as entrepreneurs or venture capitalists and apply some of the same principles they used in business to their giving. Many are often committed to a cause or social issue more than to a single institution and support organizations that can have an impact on that cause. They prefer supporting new ideas or programs that advance social change rather than the traditional campaign priorities of endowment and bricks and mortar. They want measurable impact and condition their support on the organization meeting agreed-upon milestones or metrics. And perhaps their defining characteristic is that they want to be involved and have influence beyond financial support. They bring their ideas and talents as well as their money.

There are some challenges to engaging such donors in colleges and universities, especially in campaigns. Campaigns are about the institution's own carefully considered priorities, which may not leave too much room for new ideas. The mission of higher education—the creation and transmission of knowledge—does not directly address social problems in the way that many nonprofit organizations do. The bureaucracy and culture of higher education, and the institution of tenure, may limit the ability of a college or university to be flexible and responsive to innovative ideas or to share power with outsiders. For that reason, many entrepreneurial donors have preferred to establish their own foundations or organizations or to become involved with those in which they may exercise more influence. The definition of appropriate performance metrics for higher education also is more complicated than, for example, measuring the high school graduation rates of young people who participate in an after-school tutoring program. The benefits are long term, so it may be more difficult for an entrepreneurial donor to identify exactly what impact occurred because of his or her support.

I have met a number of entrepreneurial donors, both as a university development officer and as a consultant interviewing donors to other nonprofit organizations. I remember in particular a conversation with a venture capitalist that I conducted as part of a study for a nonprofit organization, which I will refer to as "the opera" in order to preserve its anonymity (it was not the opera). His view and approach made him for me a kind of archetype. He was frank, saying, "I'm not very interested in the opera or other traditional institutions." He was interested in organizations that were helping provide opportunities for low-income children. He explained, "My parents supported things like operas and universities. They had witnessed the destruction of institutions in Europe during World War II and, for them, the opera house, the symphony hall, libraries, university campuses, and institutions like that were symbols of what had been lost. So they directed their philanthropy to assure that such institutions would be maintained as the foundation of civilized society.

"For my generation," he continued, "the formative event was the Watts riots in Los Angeles, where I grew up, in 1965. That shaped my thinking about society and giving. I don't question the importance of traditional institutions, but they have plenty of money. What's core for me is assuring that young people born into poverty have an opportunity to get out and it is to programs that address that goal that I give my support." It is, of course, easy to understand how his experiences affected his thinking and difficult to argue with his priorities.

With regard to the high-engagement of donors, some ask, "Is this really something new?" Surely, highly engaged donors are not a completely new phenomenon—many major donors are and always have been among the most engaged members of any institution's constituency. Some point to the close involvement of Leland Stanford, and his wife, in the details of construction and faculty hiring at the university that bears their name. John D. Rockefeller also played a hands-on role in the building of Spelman College, down to the design of campus landscaping (Allen, 2002). Of course, what was different then was that those were indeed new institutions. Most colleges and universities now are long established and are sophisticated about strategic planning for their own futures, perhaps providing less opportunity for a similar level of engagement by their benefactors in core matters. So, the second question becomes whether the innovative programs that have been developed to engage entrepreneurial donors may build relationships with those individuals that eventually will lead to more traditional support of college and university priorities.

Some universities have developed approaches to engaging entrepreneurial donors and some successes are reported. In her article, "When Venture Philanthropy Rocks the Ivory Tower," Luisa Boverini tells the story of venture philanthropist Jane Brown, who lives in Baltimore, and her involvement with her alma mater, the University of Maryland–College Park. As a member of the campus's foundation board, Brown has worked with the university to develop its Baltimore Incentive Awards, a scholarship program that supports students from nine city high schools who attend Maryland. She is a volunteer in the J-Lab, a program of the university's School of Journalism, and an interdisciplinary center called the Democracy Collaborative, which studies economic development in poor communities (Boverini, 2006, p. 96). These programs are consistent with her interest in reducing poverty in her home city and with her desire for active involvement in the activities she supports. The case provides an example of how a university with an array of programs and initiatives can connect with a donor whose priority may be the social impact of a higher education institution rather than the mission of higher education per se.

Other universities have engaged venture philanthropists by drawing on their professional expertise. For example, the UCLA Foundation solicited gifts (or investments) toward a venture fund that invests in businesses to benefit the university. The fund is managed separately from the regular endowment by a volunteer committee drawn from Silicon Valley entrepreneurs and investors (Allen, 2002). The University of California–Berkeley, Stanford, Notre Dame, DePaul, and others have programs that similarly involve alumni in managing a venture fund and/or mentoring students on starting their own businesses. George Washington University holds workshops on angel investing and invites entrepreneurial alumni, who invest $100,000, to lecture and identify opportunities for the transfer of research to commercial enterprise. They also mentor and advise faculty and students on beginning new businesses or commercializing research findings. GW's Council of Entrepreneurial Tech Transfer and Commercialization also assists other universities to develop similar initiatives (Adelman and Stanco, 2007).

What is interesting about the accounts of innovative strategies that colleges and universities have undertaken with entrepreneurial donors is that they do invoke some traditional fundraising ideas and principles. In the case of Jane Brown, reported by Boverini, the university's programs to assist students in Baltimore and study poverty reduction are consistent with the donor's priorities and thus provided a focus of her support. But, Boverini (2006) explains, Brown's relationship with College Park's president and vice president for university relations are important, too. Brown appreciates handwritten notes from the president that thank her for her work and regular communication from the vice president, who "listens" and introduces her to new initiatives that may interest her (p. 95). Augie Freda, director of development research at Notre Dame says, "Angel [investor] groups are like other cultivation activities: They provide a place for alumni to reconnect" (Adelman and Stanco, 2007). Adelman and Stanco point out that when an angel workshop leads to a new business, it may ultimately enrich the student entrepreneur, a faculty member, and the alumnus angel investor. "The university now has three development prospects," they write, "who will attribute their windfall at least partly to the entrepreneurial environment and resources of the university." They promise that, "As the alumni become more connected through the institution's entrepreneurial opportunities, the likelihood of their making a gift will increase, as with any cultivation effort" (Adelman and Stanco, 2007). That sounds not unlike a recognition of Prince and File's (1994) re-payer donor type.

Boverini (2006) advises development officers (and it would surely apply to presidents as well) to listen and carefully consider the ideas of such donors, to become "idea processors" rather than "idea generators," and to try to "craft a solution to fulfill what the venture philanthropist determines as a perceived need for the institution" (p. 98). But, she acknowledges, it may not always be possible for colleges and universities to gain the interest of entrepreneurial donors or to accommodate to their approach. She writes that "a demand for compelling near term results may be more than some institutions can handle or actually need to handle" (p. 104).

Some understand Schervish's discernment model as requiring the institution to move toward the donor's priorities. But Schervish also emphasizes the purpose of finding *convergence* between the donor's interests and the institution's priorities. Some entrepreneurial donors just may never have higher education as their principal interest; that is possibly true of my archetype venture philanthropist mentioned earlier. In some cases, as Allen describes, a college or university seeking support from a donor who comes from the entrepreneurial perspective may be "trying to jimmy the square peg of venture philanthropy into the round hole that is education" (Allen, 2002). As Boverini (2006) writes, "College and universities can, and do, turn down all kinds of offers . . . accompanied by conditions that they cannot accept or that do not fit a particular fundraising plan" (p. 104).

But it may turn out that some donors will continue to follow a venture philanthropy model with regard to some portion of their giving but also a more traditional approach with another portion, just as many individuals are stock traders with some portion of their portfolio and investors with another. There may be room for their other philanthropic interests and for their colleges and universities. (Indeed, some well-known entrepreneurial donors, including Bill Gates, have supported universities as well as their own foundations and programs.) Some donors' interests and proclivities also may evolve as they reach various stages in their own business and personal lives. As one young venture philanthropist alumnus of GW told me when I asked him to endow a professorship, "Come back and see me when I'm seventy-five." He subsequently made a major gift for current support of new programs at the university that were consistent with his other interests. He is not yet close to seventy-five. When he's seventy-five, I will be eighty-five. I plan to bring the matter to the attention of whoever is the university's chief development officer at that time!

MAKING THE ASK

This final section of the chapter goes to what some may consider the ultimate art of fundraising: the solicitation of a major campaign gift. Some who are experienced and for whom solicitation is something that comes naturally may find it too basic. For others, it may provide a structure in which to think about this important step in the fundraising process. Because it is an art, the best way to go about solicitation is not something on which all experts do agree. The principles discussed below are ones that have been effective for me and for presidents and others with whom I have worked. Some may think some of them wrong. They may be right.

Solicitation Principles

The first—and most important—principle of solicitation is that it must occur. People do not give if they are not asked, explicitly. This may seem obvious, but I have seen many situations in which relationships were well cultivated and the institution just waited for the gift to arrive. Or in which a president, development officer, or someone else visited a prospect, held a fine conversation, and left without a direct ask having been delivered. Indeed, research has determined that being asked is one of the top reasons why people who give say they do so. Those who do not often say that the reason why is that they have never been asked.

It is important that the prospect is prepared. There must be reason to think that he or she is ready to give. There has been a history of contacts and he or she probably has made previous gifts. The major gift solicitation is thus not a qualifying or discovery visit, nor is it cultivation. The cultivation has occurred and the relationship has advanced to the point that a positive response is anticipated.

Success comes from having the right people ask the right person or people for the right gift at the right time. So, determining the composition of the solicitation team is an important decision that requires thought and discussion. That subject has been discussed earlier and does not need elaboration here.

The solicitors need to decide in advance of the solicitation what they will ask and how it will be presented. In a campaign, prospects are solicited for a specific gift believed to be consistent with their financial capacity and their interests. But there are alternative ways to approach the dollar figure.

In one scenario, say, the individual being solicited has been deeply involved in campaign planning, perhaps as a member of the campaign planning committee. He or she is intimately familiar with the gift range chart for the campaign and probably has thought about where he or she needs to be in that array. In such a situation, it might be best to get to the point: "Bob, as you know, we must have two gifts at the $5 million level in order for this campaign to succeed and there are a limited number of people with the ability to provide that kind of critical leadership. We are hoping you will be able to participate at that level."

But in other situations, where the prospect may be less familiar with the mathematics of the campaign, it may be better to ask for a purpose and back into the amount rather than start with the money. For example, contrast these two (albeit extreme) approaches: "Bob, we hope you will give $5 million to the campaign, and I am sure we can figure out something that it could support that you would find interesting." Or, "Bob, one of the highest priorities for the university is to create more endowed distinguished professorships. That is essential to attracting and retaining the faculty talent we need to reach the next level of academic distinction. Is that something that you could consider?" Unless Bob is highly uninformed, which is unlikely, he will understand immediately at least the approximate range you are suggesting. But you have led with the mission and priorities, rather than a dollar sign. The question may lead Bob to ask some questions about how professorships work, how many exist now, and perhaps even more penetrating questions about the institution's academic plan. This discussion is engaging him in substance rather than merely a financial transaction. At some point he may ask, "How much would that require?" The answer would be, of course, "An endowment of $5 million." But, of course, there may be various ways in which Bob could give that amount, a point that might be explored in subsequent discussions.

The conventional wisdom is to aim high, that is, to ask for an amount that may represent a stretch for the prospect. There is wisdom in that advice, especially if the solicitors have a relatively good sense of the prospect's capability and inclination. If the initial ask is too high, it is always possible to come back with something more modest. But in my experience, there is also a risk in that approach in a situation where knowledge of the prospect may be incomplete. Asking for an amount that is clearly beyond the prospect's reach—or that does not reflect other competing interests and obligations—may be embarrassing to him or her. Even worse, it may make the solicitors look unprofessional for suggesting something so unrealistic. Negotiating down can sometimes strike a tone of desperation, as in, "Well, Bob, if you can't give the $5 million, how about 2? Okay, how about 1?" Of course, one of the benefits of asking for a purpose rather than an amount is that it makes the coming down easier without making the prospect feel that he or she has disappointed you. For example, if an endowed distinguished professorship is not of interest to Bob, there is also a critical need for more junior faculty positions and, of course, scholarships for both graduate and undergraduate students.

There are various points of view on whether a written proposal should be prepared in advance of the solicitation visit. For example, David Gearhart, a former vice president for development and a fundraising consultant, who is now chancellor of the University of Arkansas, strongly advises, "The gift amount should always be decided in advance and supported with a specific written proposal provided by the staff" (Gearhart, 2006, p. 198). There is no harm in preparing a written proposal in advance of the visit, and doing so may help to clarify the solicitors' thoughts and get the team on the same page. But the proposal should be kept in the briefcase during the conversation. It can be left behind if the conversation evolves in ways anticipated by the proposal but carried back home in the briefcase if it goes a different way. It has often been my experience that such discussions reveal new information or provide insights on the donor that should be incorporated in a written proposal. So I developed the pattern of waiting to write the proposal after the meeting and of using it as a tool for a follow-up contact.

The location of the solicitation and the participants in the meeting are variables that need to be carefully considered in advance. The ideal location varies by case, but a home or office is generally better than a restaurant or a social event. There are too many distractions in a restaurant, and the public setting is often inappropriate for discussion of such personal matters as a gift. I have too often heard a solicitor begin the ask, "Well, Betty, we are hoping you will consider . . ." only to be interrupted by, "Can I get you some dessert?" It is hard to regain the rhythm of the conversation after such a break.

Some prospects will appreciate the formality of a meeting at his or her office, but there may be others (for example, retired people) who would prefer to be visited at home. Whether the meeting should be with a prospect alone or include his or her spouse is a determination that needs to be made on the basis of what is known about the family, that is, how philanthropic decisions are made. A decision about who should be included determines in part the best location.

Wherever its location, the visit should always be scheduled and apart from other events. A side conversation at a sporting event or in the corner of a reception room or on the golf course is just about never an appropriate or effective way to solicit a major gift.

The solicitation team needs to prepare. Teams that have been working together for a long time may have their routine down, but others should not try to wing it. Some may find it useful to rehearse the visit, perhaps having someone who knows the prospect play his or her part. But others may find rehearsing to be artificial and unhelpful. At the least, there needs to be a game plan for the visit and the solicitation team should have at least one conversation about how they plan to conduct the conversation. It needs to be understood who will start the discussion, who will decide when to transition to the ask, who will decide when it is time to wrap it up, and who will suggest the next step.

ANATOMY OF THE SOLICITATION VISIT

I emphasize again that every case is different, and so there is no one magic formula for conducting a solicitation visit. But many solicitations have identifiable phases and transitions, which the following paragraphs describe.

Making the Appointment

There are different views about who should make the appointment for the visit, that is, whether the solicitor should call directly or have an assistant or staff person do so. In the case of the president, in my view, the call usually should not be made directly by the president. It may be placed by his assistant or by a development officer, who often will be talking with a staff person on the other end as well. There may be cases where the president feels it important to place the call personally, but if he or she is speaking directly with the prospect that may require some artful dodging. It is essential to avoid being pulled into the solicitation conversation on the phone.

There are various techniques for gaining appointments and a full discussion is beyond the scope of this chapter. But it is essential that the meeting be at the prospect's convenience and that the president be willing to change his or her calendar as needed. One of my professional development colleagues once reported to me that she had made an arrangement with her president to block out specific days for visits about three months in advance. The president would keep those days clear, and she was to schedule him with prospect visits on those dates. I am sure that the president was trying to be accommodating and it sounds like a reasonable approach. But, as I suspected when I heard about it, it did not work well. Inevitably, the most important prospects were available only on days that the president had not cleared, and those who were available on the president's timetable were not the most promising. Unfortunately, the president needs to be available almost whenever the most promising donor prospects are able to meet.

Of course, it is never good to sound desperate. When I arranged a visit and the donor's assistant would ask, "When is the president available," I would never answer "anytime, anywhere." I would give a more nuanced answer and turn the question around, for example, "Well, he has a very busy schedule, but there is some flexibility—what would work best for Mr. Jones?"

Opening Small Talk

The meeting begins with small talk. Most donors' offices provide some anchors—the family photos on the credenza or the model sailboat on the desk may provide clues. The weather and the news are also good starting points. But it should not go on too long and should not stray into substantive topics that may use up too much time (or lead to controversy).

Transition to Substance

If the small talk goes on too long it will eat up the appointment time; the ask and subsequent discussion may be rushed. Knowing when to jump in and redirect the conversation, to initiate a transition from small talk to the purpose of the visit, is an art. The moment must be *felt*. It usually comes at the end of some piece of small talk when there is an audible pause.

There are various phrases that can be used to signal the transition. "Bill, we appreciate your willingness to meet with us today about the college's campaign." "Tom, let me explain why we are here." "Mary, as you know, we are here to talk with you about the college and its future."

Once the transition has been made, there may be a brief summary—an elevator speech—that summarizes the priorities of the campaign and its goals. "Harry and Beth, as you know, the college has grown both in size and reputation. But we are now beginning a program that we think is essential to its future. The trustees have launched a campaign . . ."

The Ask

The substantive presentation needs to culminate in the ask! As a development officer, I once worked with a dean who was new to the job, having been appointed from a faculty position. He was far from shy and provided an articulate case for his school. But on our first few visits together, he would talk too long. The prospect was always attentive and admiring, but the meeting time would expire without an ask. The prospect would say, "Thanks for coming by," and we would depart. The dean would say to me, "I think that went well" and, indeed, in a way it had. But no gift would be forthcoming because none had been requested. After a few meetings went the same way, I needed to say, "Yes, it went great, but you never asked the prospect to give." The dean acknowledged that he found it difficult to cross the line from making the case to asking for the gift. So we worked out a routine for the next visit.

He kept making the case until I made eye contact with him. That was his cue to say, "And we're in a campaign and Mike will tell you some more about that." I picked up the conversation and proceeded to the ask. Once the barrier had been broken and the subject was on the table, the dean jumped back in and steered the discussion to closure. After that, he became quite comfortable and skilled at making the ask and did so with great success in the years that followed.

Pause and Listen

Once the ask is out, the solicitor should stop talking and listen carefully to the response. It is not usually a definitive "no way." If that occurs, there has been a serious breakdown in the evaluation of the prospect and in fundraising strategy. The response may be an enthusiastic and unconditional "yes," but more often there will be nuance.

The prospect may ask questions, to which the solicitor should respond succinctly without launching back into making the case. The prospect may raise what in sales are called objections, that is, arguments against making the gift. Sometimes this may be a verbal manifestation of the prospect's thought process, as he or she runs through the possible barriers to saying yes. The solicitor must be prepared with answers or possible solutions to these objections. That is not to say that the solicitor should become argumentative, but rather, suggest some ways in which the prospect's concerns may be addressed.

Experienced fund raisers are familiar with typical objections. Indeed, one of my humorous development colleagues at GW once suggested that we expedite visits by developing a checklist of objections that we could just give to the prospect. It included such items as "future of my business is uncertain," "have outstanding pledges to other institutions/organization," "three kids in college now," and other common concerns that prospects voice.

Of course, most objections are legitimate and should be respected. Some may be addressed through the structure of the gift, but others may require patience and consideration. Some may provide the opportunity for clarification, planning, and follow-up.

The Follow-Up

Solicitors should never conclude the visit without setting up the next step. If the response has been negative, remain upbeat and friendly and suggest a continued relationship, because things can change. If the response has been totally positive, there may still be a need to develop a memorandum of understanding, gift agreement, or some other document to formalize the commitment. That should be prepared and delivered to the donor promptly.

If the response has been tentative, that is, less than firm but with a positive tinge, there are actions that can help to move toward closure. Perhaps the next step is another visit at the prospect's office, a visit to the campus, or a second meeting including the prospect's spouse or financial adviser. That should be proposed and, if possible, scheduled before the solicitation visit ends. There may be a need to follow up with a planned giving professional, who can assist the donor in structuring the gift in a way that is compatible with his or her broader financial circumstances.

Sometimes the next step is a written proposal, to be prepared and sent to the prospect promptly. The visit might end with the solicitor saying, "Jack, we appreciate your interest in this gift. Let us prepare a written proposal to address some of the points that you raised and to summarize what we have discussed. We'll have it to you by the end of this week. Can we meet again next week to discuss any questions you may have once you've read it?" It is essential that the solicitor retain control of the next step and does not merely rely on the prospect's indefinite commitment to "get back to you."

Most major gifts require a memorandum of understanding (MOU) or gift agreement, especially if the purpose is an endowment fund that the institution will manage in perpetuity. Usually this is prepared after the donor has committed to the gift, with the purpose of formalizing the terms and establishing a guide to future management of the fund. But I sometimes have used the memorandum of understanding as a tool for moving a gift toward closure. If the meeting ends with the prospect favorably inclined, but not firm, I might skip the proposal and go right to the MOU. I might say something like, "Elaine, I think the scholarship fund in memory of your parents could be meaningful to you, and it certainly would be important to the university and students. Let me take a shot at drafting a memorandum describing how it would work—just a draft. Go over it and mark it up however you want and then let's meet to talk about it again."

In this scenario, the draft MOU may be a better device than a proposal, because it is interactive. It engages the prospect not in thinking about *whether* to make the gift but about how it should be designed. As the individual marks up the draft document, perhaps suggesting new language here or there, he or she is considering questions such as, Should there be one scholarship or two? Should they be named for each of my parents or should both include both of their names? And so forth. This process of thought presumes that the gift will be made, increasing the likelihood that it will. But, this strategy must be employed carefully, lest the prospect feel rushed or perceive it as a premature push to get a signature on a legal document.

This chapter began by stating that fundraising solicitation is an art that requires insight, intuition, and judgment. Listening and observing a prospect's reaction to an ask, evaluating his or her true inclinations and desires, and judging when to move forward and when to pull back are essential skills.

GIFT PLANNING

This book does not include a detailed discussion of planned giving or gift planning. Indeed, it is a complex subject that itself fills volumes. But neither do presidents—or most development officers—need to know much more than the basics. They need to know enough about the most common instruments (for example, bequests, charitable gift annuities, charitable remainder trusts) to recognize a scenario in which planned giving may provide a vehicle for a donor to fulfill the desire to give. A planned giving professional can work out the details with the donor or with the donor's advisers.

Three variables are most relevant in identifying a planned giving scenario: the nature of the donor's assets, the donor's general attitudes toward money, and the donor's family and life circumstances. For example, a donor with highly appreciated assets, such as stocks or real estate, may benefit from a giving method that avoids tax on capital gains. Some donors may have assets but exhibit a cautious approach to money. They may be reluctant to accept the risk in a charitable remainder trust but may find comfort in the regular income that a gift annuity can provide. Planned giving also may provide a solution for those who are concerned about the financial security of a spouse, family member, or partner, but some instruments will do so better than others. Some of these concerns may be objections that donors will raise. Solicitors need to be sufficiently familiar with the tool kit of planned giving to identify a situation in which the follow-up should move in that direction. They are common in campaigns today.

REFERENCES

Adelman and Stanco. (2007). "A Match Made in Heaven" [electronic verson]. *Currents*, October, 2007. www.case.org (accessed November 13, 2009).

Allen, Kent. (2002). "The Mechanics of Venture Philanthropy" [electronic version]. *Currents*, November/December. www.case.org (accessed July 21, 2009).

Boverini, Luisa. (2006). "When Venture Philanthropy Rocks the Ivory Tower." *International Journal of Educational Advancement* 6, no. 2 (February), pp. 84–106.

Dunlop, David R. (2002). "Major Gift Programs." In Michael J. Worth (Ed.), *New Strategies for Educational Fund Raising*. Westport, CT: American Council on Education and Praeger, pp. 89–104.

Gearhart, G. David. (2006). *Philanthropy, Fundraising, and the Capital Campaign: A Practical Guide*. Washington, DC: National Association of College and University Business Officers.

Prince, Russ Alan, and Karen Maru File. (1994). *The Seven Faces of Philanthropy*. San Francisco: Jossey-Bass.

Rhodes, Frank H. T. (Ed.). (1997). *Successful Fund Raising for Higher Education*. Phoenix: American Council on Education and the Oryx Press.

Schervish, Paul G. and John J. Havens. (2002). "The New Physics of Philanthropy: The Supply-Side Vectors of Charitable Giving. Part II: The Spiritual Side of the Supply Side." *CASE International Journal of Educational Advancement* 2, no. 3 (March), pp. 221–241.

8

Post-Campaign Evaluation, Planning, and Stewardship

The campaign ends with the victory celebration. Like the kickoff, it is often a major event, accompanied by broad communication to inform the entire constituency about the successful completion of the campaign and its impact on the programs of the college or university.

The victory celebration and related communications recognize major donors and campaign volunteers and report the impact of campaign gifts—new professorships created, scholarships awarded, and facilities constructed or improved. That impact is best communicated through human stories rather than a mere financial summary. Such stories may describe the research or innovative teaching of a professor newly appointed to an endowed position, a student who was able to complete his or her education because of a scholarship received, or the expansion of a department into new or renovated space. The recognition of campaign donors also can include their stories, that is, a description of their relationships with the college or university and the motivations behind their gifts.

Recognition and credit for the campaign's success should be broadly and generously dispensed, including volunteers who served on campaign committees but whose performance perhaps left something to be desired. Expressions of gratitude are free and some of them may do more in the future.

There may be a single large event to mark the completion of the campaign, but the most magical moments may come in more focused events that recognize individual donors. One might be a small dinner for a donor couple and their friends and families, perhaps held in the building named for them. Another might be a lunch at which the donor meets the students receiving the scholarship he or she endowed or the professor who has been appointed to an endowed chair. In some cases, recognizing some donors at events in their home communities, where family and friends can easily attend, may be preferable to on-campus events populated by college or university staff. Most donors derive great satisfaction and emotional pleasure from such small and personalized experiences, which may help them to *feel* the impact of their gift.

POST-CAMPAIGN ANALYSIS AND PLANNING

Most institutions publish a campaign final report—a formal printed and/or electronic piece that lists campaign volunteers and donors and includes articles highlighting key gifts. Many also undertake a detailed analysis and evaluation of the campaign and some engage a fundraising consultant to do so. The post-campaign evaluation may be nearly as extensive as a feasibility study and may analyze, among other points,

- commitments to the campaign by gift level, compared with the gift range chart anticipated in the campaign plan (this can highlight areas of under- or over-performance and provide lessons for efforts going forward);
- commitments by source (individual, corporation, foundation), compared with projections made at the beginning of the campaign;
- commitments by impact, that is, current and deferred gifts;
- increases in annual giving, in dollars and participation, over the campaign period;
- goal attainment by priority and objective;
- new prospects identified and developed during the campaign;
- analysis of planned giving in the campaign and projections of planned gift revenue in future years;
- the cost-effectiveness of campaign initiatives and of each solicitation program; and
- evaluation of staff and volunteer organization and structure.

There are also qualitative indicators that should be examined, for example,

- impact of the campaign on institutional visibility and reputation;
- impact of the campaign on the culture of philanthropy among the institution's constituents; and
- impact of the campaign on the culture of fundraising on campus, among unit leaders, faculty, and others.

Whether the post-campaign analysis and report is prepared by a consultant or by institutional staff, it serves some important purposes. Among others, it documents institutional memory, provides a guide to successors who may manage the next campaign, serves as a tool for internal communication, and may uncover some loose ends from the campaign that can be leveraged into additional gifts in post-campaign fundraising. The latter may include, for example, donors who were not ready to give in the campaign's early stages but whose situations have changed and others whose campaign commitments are nearly fulfilled and who thus may be ready for an additional gift.

Post-Campaign Plans and Priorities

Results of the post-campaign analysis can provide a basis for developing a post-campaign fundraising plan. This plan will reflect the priorities and needs of each institution, but many include

- a renewed emphasis on the annual fund and alumni relations programs;
- strengthening ongoing major gifts and planned giving programs;
- developing focused campaigns or programs to address campaign subgoals that may not have been achieved or new priorities that have emerged over the course of the campaign;
- restructuring and refocusing of the fundraising professional staff;
- redefining the role of the board development or advancement committee; and
- strengthening of stewardship, donor relations, and development communications programs.

As noted earlier, it is typical that comprehensive campaigns will go over the goal for certain priorities or objectives but come up short with regard to others. Remaining objectives may be packaged into focused campaign efforts, for example, perhaps to complete the funding for certain facilities projects or to increase endowment supporting specific academic units or fields.

Or conditions may dictate new priorities for fundraising in the post-campaign environment. Increasing endowment for scholarships is a common post-campaign priority for major gifts for various reasons. It is a continuing need and one that may be attractive to donors outside of the campaign mode. It is a purpose well suited to planned giving and thus gifts can be solicited with reference to the donor's timetable and situation absent a campaign deadline. Scholarships are scalable, meaning that gifts at various levels can be accepted and managed. For example, after completing its $230 million campaign in 2006, Swarthmore College focused its fundraising on a "$20 Million/2010 Initiative" to secure additional scholarship endowment, and also increased the goals for annual giving to support scholarship awards (Swarthmore College, 2009). An initiative is not quite a campaign, but neither does it suggest a casual approach to post-campaign fundraising.

Increased scholarship support became a priority for many colleges and universities, both in campaigns and post-campaign, in the recession that began in 2007. Cornell, in the midst of a $4 billion campaign, in 2008 increased the campaign's goal for undergraduate scholarships from $225 million to $350 million (Cornell University, 2009). Barnard College introduced its Barnard Fund Scholars program, matching donors with specific students to whom they would provide current-use scholarship support (Barnard College, 2007). Having raised $145 million in its campaign concluded in 2008 (against a goal of $115 million), Ithaca College used its website to offer suggestions for post-campaign gifts, including scholarships for students and remaining naming opportunities in its new athletics and events center (Ithaca College, 2009).

If the college or university has an academic or strategic plan that looks out beyond the campaign, a plan focused on its priorities may guide fundraising in post-campaign years. There will continue to be priorities and an ongoing focus on performance. Most critically, the end of the campaign cannot be permitted to create a lull. The institution needs to continue moving forward to expand its prospect base, engage volunteer leadership, and meet its ongoing funding needs—during whatever hiatus there may be until it begins planning for the next campaign. With staff, volunteers, and donors possibly exhausted and a little bored with campaign themes, the end of the campaign is a time that calls for presidential vision and perhaps a revisiting of communication and marketing goals across the institution.

Development staff leadership may change at the end of a campaign, although that is neither required nor universal and some chief development officers serve their institutions through multiple campaigns over a long span of years. It is, however, common for more junior members of the staff to move to positions elsewhere at the end of a campaign. Campaigns are career makers, and those who have worked effectively in such an effort will often find abundant opportunities to continue their careers in higher positions at other institutions planning a campaign.

The job market for development professionals varies with the economy, but demand has been high in recent years, especially for those with campaign experience. Almost a third of fundraising professionals stay at their institutions less than three years, resulting in a loss of institutional knowledge and continuity in donor relationships (Strout, 2007). Some universities have experimented with retention bonuses to keep staff onboard for the duration of a campaign, but retaining them past the end of a campaign usually involves more than money, including, for example, opportunities for professional growth and advancement, job rotation to avoid boredom and burnout, and involvement of even junior staff in post-campaign planning (Fernandez, 2007).

Presidents surely are not required to leave at the conclusion of a campaign, but, as noted in the first chapter of this book, the average campaign roughly coincides with the average tenure of a president, about 8.5 years in 2008 (American Council on Education, 2008). Leadership of a successful campaign may indeed result in the attention of presidential search consultants, who may suggest new opportunities to presidents in such a situation. Unlike corporations, in which the successor CEO is often appointed from within, presidents and chief development officers are usually recruited from outside. Those changes can be disruptive to donors' relationships with their institutions, at least in the short run, and it is a responsibility of every president to engage in succession planning, even if he or she has no immediate plans to move. That includes assuring that donors have multiple relationships with individuals on the board and on campus, that development records and systems are thorough and encompass a detailed history of donor relationships, and that the successes and disappointments of the completed campaign are analyzed and well documented.

ACCOUNTABILITY AND STEWARDSHIP

Accountability and stewardship are not campaign-specific activities, rather they are integral components of the major gifts cycle described in chapter 6. But a campaign brings new gifts and donors and increases the need for stewardship initiatives, systems, and staff. That is especially true for gifts that have created endowment funds.

Stewardship encompasses both continuing management of the relationship with the donor as well as accountability for the impact of the gift. It is thus not only a responsibility of the development office but of the entire institution, requiring the participation of financial and investment officers, academic officers and faculty, and development professionals. Communication and common understanding between the development office and other administrative units has historically been a problem. The development office's priority is, of course, to maintain the relationship with a donor, but other offices may sometimes find that the work required of them in order to keep donors well informed is additive to their normal workload and not directly relevant to their purposes. Many institutions have improved coordination across campus through the introduction of new information and reporting systems, but gaps—and sometimes interoffice tensions—still exist.

At the heart of accountability is the prudent management of endowment funds and the assurance that income is being used in accordance with the donor's intentions. In independent colleges and universities, management of the endowment is usually carried out somewhere other than the development office, but institutionally related foundations at public colleges and universities combine fundraising and fund-management responsibilities under one entity. The institution's president needs to be engaged with the foundation's leadership as well as the governing board of the college or university, in order to assure sound practices in investment as well as donor relations.

Endowment management is governed by state law and in many states the law has changed. The Uniform Management of Institutional Funds Act set the requirements for management in most states for many years. Its restriction that institutions not spend when an endowment fell below "historic dollar value," essentially the original gift, presented some real challenges in the early 2000s. The stock market decline following the dot.com bust and 9/11 left many recently created endowments "under water," meaning that it was not legally permissible to use the endowment to support scholarships, research, or other programmatic purposes. That situation obviously created some difficult communications with donors, who wished to see the impact of their giving right away. A new model act, called the Uniform Prudent Management of Institutional Funds Act, was introduced in 2006 and has been adopted by most states (as of 2009). It permits spending from underwater endowments, but it requires that trustees (or foundation directors) exercise "the care an ordinary prudent person in a like position would exercise under similar circumstances" (Griswold and Jarvis, 2009). The new law provides greater flexibility, but it does not eliminate the need for detailed, open, and sometimes difficult communication with endowment donors whose funds may not have grown as anticipated.

Donor Relations and Communications

Many institutions have invested substantially in strengthening donor relations and communications staffs and systems in the past decade. This reflects expectations for greater accountability and communication from donors as well as the realization that donors are the institution's best prospects for future gifts. It is common practice to send endowment donors an annual report that reflects the history of the fund created with their gifts. These reports resemble those sent by an investment firm or retirement plan and show opening principal, gifts added and funds expended during the year, investment gains and losses, closing principal, and other relevant numbers. The financial report may be accompanied by a narrative summary of what was accomplished during the year with expenditures from the endowment, for example, student scholarships awarded or the research of the incumbent of an endowed professorship.

Some institutions have produced books listing all endowment funds and their purposes, which may include the profiles of donors. These can be effective vehicles not only for recognizing donors but for inspiring ideas among others who may be prospects for future gifts. The latter may include the family of endowment donors, who may wish to add to an existing fund to increase its impact and perpetuate a family tradition. Other institutions are making effective use of electronic media. For example, the University of Texas at Austin has created "Donor Direct," an online stewardship tool that provides financial information on endowed funds as well as updated information on each fund's impact. The system generates e-mails to students and professors who have benefited from the fund, prompting them to enter messages for the donors regarding their activities. The donors can access the page to read these materials, providing timely and continuing communication that may lead to additional gifts. The website supplements but does not replace traditional letters and other communications to donors from those on the campus who receive support from endowment funds (Schubert, 2005). Some donors are not yet comfortable with electronic media, and more traditional methods of communicating with them are still required, although that is likely to become less true in the future.

Of course, there is no substitute for personal interactions between people—and probably never will be. Major donors generally enjoy meeting the people whose work they have advanced. There can be risks as well as rewards in arranging such occasions. One donor in my experience had pursued a long career as an executive at the *Washington Post* and endowed an undergraduate scholarship at The George Washington University, which she had attended on a scholarship years before. (She was a definitive repayer, as discussed in chapter 7.) With inadequate preparation, I invited the first recipient of the scholarship, a freshman, to have lunch with the donor and me at the faculty club. It started out well—the student was a bright and articulate young woman—but things deteriorated when the conversation turned to the donor's career (which I think I had prompted her to describe). The student became somewhat argumentative, taking issue with investigative reporting by the *Washington Post* and, indeed, with the values and integrity of the news media generally, which she viewed as undermining all things right and good. It was a little awkward! After the lunch, when the student had departed, I took the donor aside and apologized. With a smile, she just said, "Well, it's nothing I haven't heard before. And she seemed like a bright young woman." Thankfully, she continued to add to the scholarship fund in the years ahead, and I introduced her to other scholarship recipients—who were interviewed by a member of my staff prior to arranging the lunch!

Another notable donor I knew also was a woman. She was widowed and had no children of her own; indeed, no close family members living. She also had created scholarships, and we introduced her to the first recipient. It went so well that she continued to add to the fund and there were many additional recipients in following years. She began to speak about scholarship recipients from previous years, and it was obvious that she was staying updated on their activities. She would sometimes call to ask for one of their addresses and, we learned, some came to visit her when they were in town. The donor did not have a computer, but we created a file of 3 × 5 index cards with the names and addresses of all the students who had received her scholarships. It became an annual tradition that a member of the development staff would drive to the woman's home, pick up the card file, update it with current information, and return it to her. She was delighted and used the file to maintain an active correspondence with the dozens (perhaps by now hundreds) of former students whom she had helped.

Returning to a point I made earlier in this book, for many donors a major gift may be not only rewarding, but one of the best decisions they will ever reach. Through her giving, this donor created a large family that enriched her life and the lives of the young people who joined it over the years. Today, the information system might be a website rather than a card file, but the human principles remain the same. People give to people. People may not seek, but generally appreciate, recognition. They may not request, but warmly receive, expressions of gratitude. Giving offers them opportunities to express their connectedness with the larger human community and to advance the lives of others. Colleges and universities, especially, provide the opportunity to reach across generations and positively influence both individual lives and the future of society. By nature, people will repeat actions that bring them satisfaction and feel resentful if their gifts are taken for granted or misapplied. Good stewardship requires a systematic and professional effort, but the reasons why it is important are really not that complicated.

REFERENCES

American Council on Education. (2008). "American College President Study." www.acenet.edu/Content/NavigationMenu/ProgramsServices/CPA/Executive_Summary.htm (accessed November 10, 2008).

Barnard College. (2007). "Leadership Gifts: Student Support." www.barnard.edu/giving/studentsupport.html (accessed July 29, 2009).

Cornell University. (2009). "Scholarship Aid." www.campaign.cornell.edu/scholarship-aid.cfm?v=5 (accessed July 29, 2009).

Fernandez, Kim. (2007). "Campaign Fatigue Syndrome" [electronic version]. *Currents.* www.case.org (accessed July 28, 2009).

Griswold, John, and William Jarvis. (2009). "Underwater Funds: UPMIFA Throws a Lifeline to Drowning Endowments" [electronic version]. *Currents*, July/August. www.case.org (accessed July 28, 2009).

Ithaca College. (2009). "Making the Most of Your Gift." www.ithaca.edu/giving/yourgift/index.php (accessed July 29, 2009).

Schubert, Frank D. (2005). "Present and Accounted For" [electronic version]. *Currents*, April. www.case.org (accessed July 28, 2009).

Strout, Ellen. (2007). "Colleges Try New Tactics to Retain Fund Raisers." *Chronicle of Higher Education* 54, no. 7 (October 12), p. A1.

Swarthmore College. (2009). "The $20 Million/2010 Initiative." www.swarthmore.edu/x25417.xml (accessed July 28, 2009).

9

Campaign Communications and Events

The first chapter of this book explained that "campaigns have become about more than money, often encompassing important goals related to institutional image, visibility, and brand." Institutional communications and marketing are, of course, large topics beyond the scope of this book. But this chapter briefly considers some points related to the campaign, including the development of the campaign communications plan, campaign themes and messages, core campaign publications and presentations, the campaign on the Web, and campaign events. To gain maximum advantage from a campaign, a college or university must integrate all of its communications across all the channels and media through which it interacts with the outside world. And campaign communications should reflect the core strategic directions of the institution. Achieving this integration may be easier for some institutions than for others and it is an important matter that may deserve the president's time and attention.

Smaller institutions may have a single vice president for advancement whose responsibilities encompass communications and marketing, alumni relations, and fundraising. Some larger universities, however, will have separate vice presidents responsible for fundraising and the campaign and for communications and marketing. While planning may achieve integration of visual elements and messages, there will always be competing demands for resources, time, and attention. That will require the creation of staff within the development or campaign office to focus exclusively on campaign-related communications, within the context of an integrated plan across the institution.

The campaign communications plan is developed in the campaign planning phase, and communications costs may be a substantial portion of the campaign budget. The communications plan will follow the phases of the campaign—quiet phase, kickoff, public phase, victory celebration, and the transition to post-campaign fundraising. For example, communication prior to the quiet phase may focus on institutional planning, emerging priorities, and the vision for the future. During the quiet phase, messages may remain vague about the ultimate goal of the campaign, but begin to build excitement and momentum. Saving the announcement of advance gifts for the kickoff may achieve maximum impact, but some may need to be announced during the quiet phase. Donors may not wish to wait, news about the gift may travel through informal channels, and some gifts are just rather visible by their nature.

Communications surrounding the kickoff are intense and may include many of the activities described in chapter 3—the kickoff event itself, as well as related articles and releases concerning advance gifts announced, volunteer leaders, and key priorities of the campaign. The public phase includes regular and continuing communication of progress toward the goal and the strategic announcement of gifts. The campaign's conclusion and the victory celebration require another intensive series of events and communications and then implementation of a plan for the post-campaign period that makes clear the need for continuing support.

NAMING THE CAMPAIGN

Naming the campaign is an important exercise, since the name will be highly visible for several years. It is one that also may occupy the development and communications staff and institutional and campaign leaders for hours of discussion. The choice should be informed by reflection on the institution's traditions, history, and direction as well as market research—rather than just a clever idea conceived by any particular individual.

Many campaigns take a simple approach, for example, "The Campaign for [institution name]." That is a serviceable campaign name, but it may not evoke emotion and it does not say anything about the institution's strengths or priorities. Other campaign names involve more lofty phrases, which are sometimes a source of humor. In 1979, Bernice Thieblot, founder and president of the North Charles Street Design Organization, developed an amusing menu of phrases from which campaign names might be assembled. It was so popular that it has been reprinted at least three times, including in 2004 (Thieblot, 2004). Table 9.1 includes an excerpt from a longer list that illustrates the point: just pick any infinitive from column A, combine with any phrase from column B, and add a noun from column C and you have a campaign name that is much like many that are used. The words are generically inspirational, but also convey little about a specific

Table 9.1. Campaign Name Menu

Column A	Column B	Column C
Toward	Greater	Endowment
Honoring	a Tradition of	Learning
Quest for	a Commitment to	Quality
Time for	a Heritage of	Enrichment
In Support of	the Enrichment of	Leadership
Celebrating	a Century of	Service
Opportunity for	a Larger	Purpose
Creating	a More Perfect	Wisdom
To Share	an Ancient	Gift
Burnishing	a Hallmark of	Tradition
To Sustain	a Renowned	Difference
To Perpetuate	a Signal	Presence
In Search of	a Mighty	History
Fulfilling	a Grand	Promise
Resources for	the Vastness of	Edifice
Generating	the Elements of	Excellence
Ennobling	A Capacity for	Investment
Strengthening	a Generous	Expansion
Renewing	a Tower of	Truth
Preserving	a Viable	Alternative

SOURCE: Excerpted from Thieblot, Bernice. (2004). "Name That Campaign III: New Choice for the New Millennium" [electronic version]. *Currents,* March. www.case.org (accessed July 29, 2009). Bernice Thieblot is the founder and president of North Charles Street Design Organization.

institution or its strategic or academic objectives and contribute little to larger branding and communications goals.

It would be unfair to offer examples of current campaigns that seem to follow that approach, but there are some that provide especially positive examples. That is, they are campaign names that derive from and communicate the mission, strengths, traditions, and priorities of the college or university and provide a shorthand statement of the case. For example, "Knowledge for the World," the name of Johns Hopkins's campaign, initiated in 2000 and completed in 2008, is consistent with the university's position as a leading research institution that, indeed, contributes new knowledge to the world. Dartmouth's $1.3 billion "Campaign for the

Dartmouth Experience" has a good name, consistent with the student-fo-
cused campaign priorities of education, residential and campus life, and
financial aid (Dartmouth College, 2009). Cornell's campaign, "Far Above:
The Campaign for Cornell," combines the generic "Campaign for . . ." with
a phrase that has a double meaning. It is, of course, from the title of Cornell's alma mater ("Far above Cayuga's Waters") and thus may evoke the
sentiment of graduates, but it is also consistent with one of the campaign's
priorities: "to make Cornell the best of its kind, a beacon among the world's
leading universities. We want Cornell—the first truly American university—to lead as a model for all of higher education, into this new century"
(Cornell University, 2009).

When there is a clear line from strategic priorities of the college or university to the name and themes of the campaign and the integration of campaign themes and messages with communications and marketing across the
institution, synergies are created that benefit fundraising as well as overall
institutional branding.

In a 2007 article, Robert Moore, managing partner of the marketing
communications firm Lipman Hearne, made the point that "campaigns
are opportunities to define, position, and enhance campus brands" and
raised the questions: "Does the institutional brand come first, serving as a
springboard for the campaign brand? Or does the campaign brand come
first and propel the institutional brand forward in new and exciting ways?"
His conclusion was that it may happen either way, depending on timing,
but that in ideal circumstances, "Institutional brands and campaign brands
. . . work in concert" (Moore, 2007). "People don't give to the campaign,
they give to the institution," Moore argued.

> Therefore, the institutional brand—how people feel about it, how they per-
> ceive it, how they define it, how they position it relative to their other inter-
> ests—remains the primary lodestone for the campaign brand. But the institu-
> tional brand, by itself, isn't enough to energize a campaign. Campaign brands
> must resonate with and challenge institutional brands because no one gives
> mega gifts to sustain the status quo. Campaign branding must push beyond
> the immediate value proposition into the potential impact of the institution
> after it has achieved its campaign goals, all the while still passing the sniff test
> for the people who know and love the institution. (Moore, 2007)

Moore provides four case studies to illustrate his points. The University
of Miami's $1 billion "Momentum: The Campaign for the University of
Miami" used a bold identity mark and campaign materials that reflected the
energy and dynamism of the institution and its home city. Brown's $1.4 bil-
lion campaign, announced in 2005, was named "Boldly Brown: The Campaign for Academic Enrichment." The name and related elements captured

both the president's vision for academic excellence as well as the pride of alumni. "Boldly Brown" became a theme incorporated in the university's general communications. The theme "Something Great in Mind" was developed to help differentiate the University of Wisconsin–Milwaukee from the more visible institution in Madison. It provided the basis for institutional branding and was later carried over as the theme of the campus's campaign, launched in 2006. For Denison University, the phrase "Higher Ground" provided a theme for institutional branding as well as a $160 million campaign. As Moore explains,

> "Higher Ground" works on many levels. First, it reinforces Denison's primary attribute: a sense of aerie, a remembrance of that special place where alumni spent their formative years. It also expresses an aspiration for the institution: We are not content with the status quo, but are taking Denison to new heights. (Moore, 2007)

The most effective campaign names and themes thus are those that tap the institution's true and real identity, reflect its well-considered strategic directions and priorities, and are consistent with the messages it delivers through its total communications and marketing effort. When such integration is achieved, the campaign can be, indeed, about more than money; it can provide a comprehensive strategy for advancing the college or university.

CAMPAIGN COMMUNICATION MATERIALS

Like Mark Twain's statement that reports of his death had been greatly exaggerated, predictions of a paperless world have been, at least, premature. We are living in a period of transition, perhaps, between print and new media. Campaign communications still require printed materials, but also the intensive use of electronic media, including e-mail, the Web, and social networks.

There are still donors who would prefer to read about the campaign in hard copy, and printed materials still offer some advantages. They provide physical substance, which may help to make the campaign real and tangible. (As a vice president for development, I was known for saying that I wanted the brochure to make a "thud" when it landed on a desk or coffee table.) Printed materials have a long life; they can remain on the desk or coffee table for a long time, perhaps to catch the eye and invite review on multiple occasions. And the medium may invite more reflective consideration than the computer screen, perhaps one explanation for why hard-copy books still sell. But, to emphasize, the impact of electronic media is revolutionary and campaigns today make full use of it. That is likely to be increasingly true.

A package of basic campaign materials—perhaps produced in both print and electronic format—might include the following:

The Campaign Brochure

Chapter 4 made the distinctions among the case for support, the internal case statement, and the external case statement (or campaign brochure). In practice, however, many people do refer to the brochure as "the case statement" or the "case book." It is usually a substantial and colorful piece, with inspirational copy. It spells out the priorities, objectives, and goals of the campaign in detail alongside four-color photographs of the campus and people. Because it is a substantial publication, it is not intended for broad distribution, but rather as a leave-behind publication to be used in connection with a personal visit or perhaps to accompany a written proposal.

Some argue that too much money is spent on case statements prepared at the outset of the public phase, which quickly become obsolete as the campaign evolves. (I must confess that I once sent a member of my staff to quietly clear out a couple thousand from a storage room about two years into a campaign—by which time they had become quite obsolete—to assure that no one would discover how many had in fact gone unused.) But, in my experience, few donors have ever questioned the cost of the campaign brochure and, indeed, some might find an inexpensive piece to be inconsistent with the quality and ambition that the college or university should represent.

There are some creative approaches that address the obsolescence issue. A modular case statement can include basic and non-time-sensitive information on the campaign combined with the flexibility to add or update to incorporate new needs or to address the focused interests of specific prospects. Communications professionals Roger Sametz and Tamsen McMahon, former director of development communications at the Harvard Medical School, describe an interesting approach to a modular case statement used at Harvard. Campaign priorities are organized under categories of impact, aligned with donors' perspectives. Those categories include

- influence (for donors who want to advance research in a specific disease area);
- efficiency (for donors who want to build or acquire new technologies);
- acquisition (for donors who want to support basic research);
- delivery (for donors interested in the curriculum, faculty training, and student aid); and

- transformation (for donors who want to bring about significant change in medicine and health). (Sametz and McMahon, 2009)

Fund raisers are able to assemble communication pieces, both printed and electronic, to fit the circumstances of each prospect and to be consistent with the school's priorities. In other words, "By thinking about . . . funding priorities in the context of (the five impact) categories, you can create a set of main messages and greatly increase your ability to connect with donors and prospective donors in a meaningful way. You can be donor-focused *and* mission-centric" (Sametz and McMahon, 2009, p. 44). That is a good place to be, especially with the growing numbers of entrepreneurial-type donors and the requirements of accountability and stewardship discussed in chapter 8.

The Mini-Brochure

Given the cost of the campaign brochure, it is appropriate to produce it in limited quantity for use with major gift prospects. It is often useful to produce a smaller version of the campaign brochure—more or less an abstract—which may be more suitable for mailing or for distribution at large-scale events.

Campaign Newsletter

News of campaign progress and important gifts need to be regularly reported to external constituencies through some type of publication, usually a newsletter, which of course, may be printed and/or electronic. The campaign may also be reported through existing communication vehicles, for example, a campus magazine. But the development office needs to control at least one regular publication that is focused entirely on the campaign.

Campaign Bulletins and Reports

It is essential to communicate the campaign's progress to internal constituencies, including faculty and staff and campaign volunteers. That may require a separate publication that takes a somewhat different tone and focus from what is sent to people off campus.

Videos

A campaign video cannot replace personal contact, but it can convey the emotion of the campaign in strong images. It is often unveiled at the kickoff and used effectively to set the tone for other campaign events. Some institutions have also succeeded by mailing a CD to prospects in advance of a phone solicitation and some have campaign videos on their websites.

Annual Fund Materials

Materials for the annual fund are, of course, produced with the annual cycle of solicitation. During the campaign period, they often incorporate the campaign logo and overall design elements.

Specialized Brochures

The campaign communications plan should anticipate the need for a family of printed materials, including, for example, separate brochures on key campaign objectives (perhaps professorships, scholarships, facilities projects) or on academic units (e.g., the law school, the business school, the college of arts and sciences). Planned giving requires a collection of brochures with information on various topics. Some of the needs for specialized materials may be identified in campaign planning, but it is prudent to maintain a budget for producing new materials along the way as new communication needs are identified.

Other Specialized Materials

There are a variety of materials that may be used to promote the campaign, and creativity is the only limit. For example, one institution that I attended sends me a self-mailer every now and then to announce a major gift to its campaign. It includes a description of the gift and its purposes, photos and the background of the donor, and some quotes from the donor about why he or she made the gift. It does not solicit a gift, but it does catch my attention; since it is not in an envelope, it receives at least a momentary view even if it is subsequently discarded. Sometimes the donor is a person I have known; those receive a longer look. The power of example is worth engaging, but it is wise to mail such announcements on repeated occasions, since the message can take multiple impressions to sink in and a stream of gift announcements can create a sense of building momentum.

THE CAMPAIGN ON THE WEB

Presence of the campaign on the Web is essential, since it will be the principal means by which many people receive their information. In addition, unlike printed material, the Web provides the capacity for frequent updates at low cost and the ability to interact with prospects and donors.

There are many excellent examples of campaign websites, many of which have been sources of information for this book. In 2008, Claudia Broman, director of annual giving at Northland College in Wisconsin and a student in the master's degree program in communication arts at the University of Wisconsin–Superior, conducted a study to identify the characteristics of the best campaign websites. She identified three attributes of the most effective:

1. They are no more than two clicks away from the homepage of the institution.
2. They focus on people, not buildings.
3. Their branding is cohesive with the rest of the website and with the institution itself. (Broman, 2009)

Through interviews with development officers at institutions whose campaigns had received awards from the Council for Advancement and Support of Education, Broman also identified other factors that make a campaign website successful. Among other factors, the best sites have dynamic flexibility, including frequent updates and changes in content and structure. They emphasize message over money, including photos and stories of donors and people who benefit from their gifts. They simplify the process of making an online gift, requiring only a few clicks and simple forms. And they include a message from the president that describes the impact of the campaign (Broman, 2009, pp. 30–31).

The ultimate impact of Facebook, Twitter, and other emerging communications media on campaigns is difficult to predict. And the technology is evolving so quickly that any prediction would soon be overtaken by change. But, it is clear that campaigns—indeed, colleges and universities— must have a strong presence in such media and that their importance will grow. But, new media do not, in my opinion, invalidate the fundamental principles of human interaction that have guided communication and fundraising in the past; rather, they shift their application to a higher speed. But a full exploration of the topic is just beyond the scope of this book.

CAMPAIGN EVENTS

Campaign events are essential and can be magical times. The campaign kickoff and victory celebration, a dinner or lunch to recognize new members of a gift club, or the dedication of a building to recognize an important gift—those are occasions when sentiment flows, bonds are built, and people are inspired. But in higher education, events are appropriate for the purposes of cultivation, recognition, and stewardship and almost never for the purpose of raising money.

Inevitably, there will be volunteers and maybe some campus officials who think that holding a dinner at $500 a plate, or something similar, can produce a profit to benefit the institution while also building new relationships with the people who attend. That is almost always a poor idea. (I must add the caveat that there may be specific programs or units within an institution that may benefit from a fundraising event, for example, a clinical center within a medical center or perhaps some initiative in athletics or the arts. But in general this is not a method that is effective or efficient fundraising for colleges and universities.)

The reasons the suggestion of fundraising events comes up are twofold. First, some volunteers will have had experience with nonprofit organizations that conduct what appear to be successful fundraising events and are familiar with that method. Their estimation of success is usually exaggerated because they know only the gross proceeds of such an event and do not see the direct and indirect costs (for example, staff time and opportunity cost) of producing it. And, second, they make the assumption that those who attend such charity events indeed go on to become regular donors to the organization sponsoring the event or that colleges and universities need to engage new donors in the same way. In reality, many charity events do not produce much net revenue and those who attend often do so one time at the invitation of a friend. Those who are committed to the organization often would make a gift without the social activity. But even if such events are successful for some charities, colleges and universities have a different situation. They have natural constituencies of individuals with linkage, ability, and interest with whom long-term relationships may be cultivated, leading to major gifts. Events play a role in that process, but not as fundraisers in themselves.

REFERENCES

Broman, Claudia. (2009). "Weaving the Web into Your Campaign." *Currents*, April, pp. 28–31.

Cornell University. (2009). "The Case for a Bold Campaign." www.campaign .cornell.edu/case.cfm#1 (accessed July 29, 2009).

Moore, Robert M. (2007). "Brand Opening" [electronic version]. *Currents*, April. www.case.org (accessed July 29, 2009).

Sametz, Roger, and Tamsen McMahon. (2009). "Tools of the Trade: A Modular Communications Approach Replaces the Traditional Case Statement." *Currents*, April, pp. 43–49.

Thieblot, Bernice. (2004). "Name That Campaign III: New Choices for the New Millennium" [electronic version]. *Currents*, March. www.case.org (accessed July 29, 2009).s

Conclusion

To paraphrase Yogi Berra, predictions are difficult to make, especially when they are about the future. But I have offered them in various chapters throughout this book.

First, campaigns are likely to continue to be a principal strategy for advancing colleges and universities. The campaign is a method rooted in essential principles of human motivation and behavior. Moreover, today's campaigns are about more than the money—they are also about building visibility, understanding, and image—considerations that will become no less important for colleges and universities in the competitive decades ahead.

But fundraising will need to adapt tested models to changing realities. Those include entrepreneurial donors, generations of donors accustomed to communicating through social networking sites and other electronic means, and perhaps, new economic realities.

Bruce McClintock's predictions about campaign giving, cited in chapter 4, may turn out to be correct. That is, the era of mega-gifts may have ended with the recession in 2007 and future campaigns may need to place a greater emphasis on six-figure gifts in the middle ranges and on the annual fund. If correct, that would not be all bad. In the 1990s and 2000s, the focus on a handful of top gifts may have led higher education to de-emphasize the long term, to devote insufficient attention and resources to building the pipeline of younger alumni and donors, on whom the future of campaigns will depend. To the extent that new economic realities force us to return to more traditional assumptions about the gift range chart and the fundraising pyramid, they may indeed be helpful in the long run. If we reemphasize alumni relations and the annual fund, perhaps that may help slow or reverse the erosion of alumni participation and the increasing relative appeal of charitable causes outside of higher education that pull donors in other directions. To the extent that entrepreneurial donors force us to be more flexible and responsive and to do a better job of accountability and stewardship, they may also help us to adhere more closely to what always have been sound principles.

It is impossible to predict the economy. But one benefit of having been involved in fundraising for a long time is that experience may be a guide. In the introduction to this book, I told the story of my unusual introduction to higher education fundraising under conditions of natural disaster in 1972. That period was indeed one of stress and uncertainty for all higher education institutions. The baby boomers were passing through their undergraduate years, but demographic projections suggested that college enrollments would plummet in the future. One day a colleague gave me a copy of one of the higher education best sellers of 1971, a book entitled *The New Depression in Higher Education*, by Earl F. Cheit. It was a report of a study sponsored by the Carnegie Commission and predicted the demise of many higher education institutions, most especially independent colleges like the one at which I was then employed. It caused me to think, but fortunately, I ignored the implications and continued to pursue a higher education career. Most of the endangered institutions still survive and many continue to thrive.

In the early 1980s, around the time I left the University of Maryland to become vice president at The George Washington University, I attended a speech by a corporate CEO in Washington, DC. He delivered a bleak assessment of the future. The Japanese economic juggernaut would overtake the United States within a decade; American manufacturing would disappear; the United States was destined to become, at best, stagnant, and, at worst, a nation and society in decline. I left the speech discouraged and concerned about the future of my fundraising career, although I persisted in it.

Of course, what the speaker did not anticipate was the introduction and development, over the next two decades, of the PC, the Internet, the cell phone, global positioning systems, medical advances such as cardiac bypass surgery, and many other innovations—all of them either invented or developed in the United States. New industries were created, new and unprecedented wealth was generated, and philanthropy grew to historic levels. Moreover, the tradition of philanthropy and the expectation that successful people give something back became an ever more central and powerful tenet of society—in the United States and, increasingly, around the world.

On the afternoon of October 19, 1987, I had arranged to be in the office of our campaign chair. He planned to make follow-up phone calls to some prospects who had been solicited but who had not yet reached a decision. I was to be there to provide him with whatever information he might need as he worked through the calls. The timing was not ideal. The stock market plummeted and lost about 23 percent of its value by the end of that afternoon, which came to be called "Black Monday." Needless to say, the phone conversations became increasingly bleak and we just quit after a few. We were both discouraged. But, of course, the market fully recovered over the following twenty-four months.

In the early 1990s, I sat at lunch with a prominent Washington, DC, real estate developer who was also an important donor to The George Washington University. We were in the midst of the savings and loan crisis and the values of commercial properties had plummeted, indeed, in many cities collapsed. "This is a depression," he told me. "The 1980s were a bubble and it has burst. This city and the country are in decline." Of course, within a decade commercial real estate had recovered, a burgeoning technology industry had developed in Washington's suburbs, and gentrification had turned many Washington neighborhoods into some of the hottest residential markets in the nation.

On the morning of September 11, 2001, I was in a television studio in northern Virginia helping to produce a training video on campaign fundraising. During a break, a young woman told us that a plane had struck the World Trade Center. We were distressed, but returned to taping a second take. She returned to tell us that another plane had hit, and I knew immediately what it was. In the days, weeks, and months that followed, stock markets plummeted and so did the nation's optimism about its future. But in the years since, we have seen again the resilience of the American economy and the spirit of the American people. Emotional wounds began slowly to heal, markets reached new highs, and, of course, then plummeted back down.

So, here we are again. I wrote this book in late 2008 and in 2009, during another period of economic distress and widespread pessimism about the future. Right now, as I write this paragraph, some banks are still staying alive on federal money, the U.S. government is the largest shareholder in General Motors, and unemployment at 10 percent. By the time the manuscript is edited, the book is produced, readers learn of it, buy it, and read it, things may have changed. Perhaps the recession that began in 2007 will be a mere memory. If so, that is good. If not, history teaches us to remain optimistic.

No year in history so far has been the last good year. All have been followed eventually by yet better times. Innovations of which most of us have not yet dreamed will change our lives in the decades ahead. New industries will be born. New fortunes will be made. The human impulse to give back, build for the future, and improve the lives of others will drive those fortunes toward philanthropic endeavors. Colleges and universities will endure and remain central to the aspirations of the students who attend them and the societies that support them. Campaigns will set and achieve higher goals. And the wise and energetic leadership of college and university presidents will continue to be central to their success.

REFERENCE

Cheit, Earl F. (1971). *The New Depression in Higher Education: A Study of Financial Aid Conditions at 41 Colleges and Universities*. New York: McGraw-Hill.

Index

About the Author

Michael J. Worth is professor of nonprofit management in the Trachtenberg School of Public Policy and Public Administration at The George Washington University, where he teaches graduate courses related to fundraising, philanthropy, and management of nonprofit organizations. He also provides fundraising and management advice to colleges and universities, national institutions and associations, and nonprofit organizations.

Dr. Worth has more than thirty-five years of experience in higher education and philanthropic resource development. He served as vice president for development and alumni affairs at The George Washington University from 1983 to 2001 and previously served as director of development at the University of Maryland–College Park. At George Washington, Dr. Worth planned and directed two major campaigns and provided support to the board of trustees for board development programs.

Dr. Worth has written or edited seven books, including *Public College and University Development* (1985), *Educational Fund Raising: Principles and Practice* (1993), *The Role of the Development Officer in Higher Education* (1994), *New Strategies for Educational Fund Raising* (2002), *Securing the Future* (2005), *Sounding Boards* (2008), and *Nonprofit Management: Principles and Practice* (2009).

He holds a B.A. in economics from Wilkes College, an M.A. in economics from The American University, and a Ph.D. in higher education from the University of Maryland–College Park.